I0425685

SOCIOLOGY, CONCEPTS OF GROUP BEHAVIOUR

ISBN: 978-1-291-51888-7

Andreas Sofroniou   2013 ©   Copyright

Andreas Sofroniou   2013 ©   Copyright

SOCIOLOGY, CONCEPTS OF GROUP BEHAVIOUR

ISBN: 978-1-291-51888-7

1

CONTENTS

1. SOCIAL STRUCTURE AND STRATIFICATION

1.1 Systematic Study

Sociology as a social science refers to the systematic study of the development, structure, and functioning of society. The late 19th-century writings of Marx, Weber, and Durkheim laid the foundations of sociology. All three analysed many facets of their own societies, in the more general context of observing the causes and consequences of the transition from traditional pre-industrial life to modern societies.

The fundamental postulate of sociology is that human beings act not by their own free decisions taken rationally, but under the influence of history and culture, and the expectations and demands of others: human beings are both the products and the makers of their societies.

Sociologists are less concerned with the characteristics of individuals than with patterns of behaviour (between doctors and patients, for instance, or priests and parishioners), which recur irrespective of the individuals involved. During the 20th century, sociologists have been particularly interested in the influence of role, status, class, and power on experience and behaviour, in the family and in the community; in the factors which contribute to cohesion and conflict; in social structure and social stratification; and in social problems such as crime, drug addiction, and domestic violence.

There are many approaches to sociology, from the functionalism of Parsons to the Marxism of the Frankfurt School. While some sociologists are primarily theorists, many analyse data gathered through interviews, observation, and surveys. Sociological findings are used increasingly by governments and businesses such as advertising and public relations.

1.2 Communication

As an academic subject, sociologists place a great importance on communication. This is interpreted as the mutual exchange of information between individuals, a process central to human experience and social organization. The study of communication involves many disciplines, including linguistics, psychology, sociology, and anthropology. All forms of communication, from interpersonal to mass media communications, involve an initiator, who formulates a message and sends it as a signal, by means of a particular channel, to a receiver, who decodes and interprets the meaning.

In interpersonal communication involving face-to-face conversation, communication is direct, using the code of language, and reinforced by non-verbal communication such as body movement, eye contact, gesture, and facial expression. Response is also direct. Interpersonal communication can also take place at a distance.

Other forms of communication use writing and printing as means of conveying messages. The invention of the printing press was the first step in the development of mass communication. Books, newspapers, and periodicals are able to convey messages to a wide audience; an even wider audience is reached by radio and television, film, and the recording industries.

The mass media and the arts impose their own codes and characteristics on to their messages, which can range from relatively straightforward ideological tracts to complex texts carrying multiple layers of possible meaning·

1.3 Founders of Sociology

The German sociologist, Max Weber (1864-1920), is considered to be one of the founders of sociology. His ideas, which spanned subjects from economic history to the sociology of music, continue to be extremely influential. Weber argued that there was a link between the emergence of Protestantism (in the 16th century) and what he termed the Protestant ethic, and the rise of capitalism.

He was one of the first to see the importance of bureaucracy, which he analysed as a form of social organization which consisted of a hierarchy of paid, clearly defined offices, filled by individuals selected on merit who were free and able to progress up the hierarchy, which itself was controlled from the top. Weber refined the analysis of social stratification, arguing, for example, that an individual's class could depend on the possession of skills as well as on property ownership and occupation, and he stressed the role of status in social inequality.

According to Weber, sociology should concern itself with the interpretation and explanation of social behaviour, not simply with its observation and description, thus distancing himself from approaches influenced by Comte's positivism. Weber was concerned with the responsibilities of the social scientist and argued for the pursuit of 'value-freedom' in academic life: personal beliefs must not interfere with investigation and analysis. Weber's major work, published posthumously, is *Economy and Society* (1922).

1.4 Philosophy of Science

In establishing sociology as a social science, philosophy can be considered as a main contributor to the investigation of the concepts and methods of the natural and social sciences. There are two major themes. Historically the most important is the realism debate which dates back to the time of the pioneer astronomer scientists Galileo (1564-1642) and Copernicus (1473-1543) and is concerned with the interpretation of scientific theories. The question is whether these theories should be regarded as true descriptions of the world (scientific realism) or whether they are rather instruments which are not literally true, but simply useful in that they enable us to make successful predictions about immediately observable phenomena (instrumentalism).

A more recent debate concerning the nature of scientific progress is the rationality debate, which asks how we can characterize the 'scientific method', or even whether such a single, universal method can be identified (see Popper). Both debates have strong links with epistemology, the theory of knowledge. On the question of scientific rationality we can ask what sort of justification there can be for the choice of one scientific theory over another. And in the realism issue, we can ask whether we have adequate justification for regarding scientific statements as literally true.

A further question is the relationship between the natural sciences (such as physics and chemistry) and the social sciences (such as economics and sociology). Should they be regarded as close enough to share the same methods (as in Comte's positivism)? Or are the methods of the natural sciences inappropriate for the subject-matter of the social sciences? Do the natural and social sciences even have the same aim? It has been argued that the aim of natural science is prediction and control of natural processes, whereas the aim of the social sciences is to understand human behaviour. The question of reductionism plays a role here: can sociology be reduced to psychology, and psychology in turn to a more physically grounded neuroscience? Or are social and psychological processes irreducible?

1.5 Social Science

In understanding sociology, one must consider it a subject within the social sciences. Sociology, therefore, is one part of the branches of the study of human society and social relationships. The disciplines usually encompassed, at least in some of their aspects, are: anthropology, demography, economics, geography, political science, psychology, and sociology.

The codification of the social sciences began in the 18th century, when the success of the natural sciences inspired the belief that humanity could be investigated similarly. Early approaches often sought to adapt to social enquiry the methods used to investigate the natural world. Laws were postulated and evidence for them sought. This approach has been called naturalism or positivism.

Such methods and views persist to the present day, and some social scientists share objectives with natural scientists. They seek to test hypotheses and to explain and predict phenomena. They use experiments and statistical techniques to establish correlations. Economists and psychologists are frequently to be found in this group. However, from the late 19th century many writers, among them, most notably, the German sociologist Weber, maintained that the social sciences could still be rigorous without copying the methods of natural science.

Rather than looking for law-like statements or working numerically, the social scientist could be more interpretive and intuitive. Social scientists following this approach tend to lay greater stress on the observation and interpretation of complex phenomena as they occur in the world rather than in experiments, and on eliciting the views of those being studied.

Anthropologists and sociologists are frequently to be found in this group. While the quantitative and qualitative approaches have different antecedents and are used for different purposes, the understanding of a phenomenon or problem often requires a combination. For example, attempts to understand, ameliorate, and prevent famines in Africa require the skills not only of economists, who analyse the effects of fluctuations in commodity prices on the ability of nations to import foodstuffs, but also of anthropologists, who investigate the ways in which farmers themselves husband their resources in a drought, thus helping aid agencies to formulate appropriate strategies.

Social scientists are found in almost every society in the world, as their work is used by governments and public and private bodies in the attempt not only to understand the world, but to master it. It is increasingly recognized that the great challenges of over-population, environmental degradation, economic revival in the former Eastern bloc and Africa, and the spread of Aids cannot be met by technical or technological solutions alone.

It is necessary to understand why people act as they do and to analyse the interaction of a multiplicity of forces. However, disagreements among social scientists in their analyses of issues and in their proposals for action, and their increasing specialization, mean that the policy-maker wishing to use social science research findings is faced with a formidable task.

1.6 Structuralism

Structuralism came to be applied to many areas, including sociology and literary criticism. From the 1960s literary structuralism flourished, particularly in France. Although it was never a unified critical school, certain ideas were predominant. If one considers sociology as a subject very much relating to philosophy, then structuralism is the method of study in which the phenomenon to be analysed is seen as comprising a system of structures, which are regarded as more important than the isolated elements that make them up.

Structuralism derives from the linguistic theories of Saussure in the early 20th century. Saussure regarded language as a vast network of structures; he broke it down into its minimal components (linguistic units such as phonemes and words), which could be defined only in relation to other such units. Saussure's linguistic theories were applied by the anthropologist Levi-Strauss in his study of myth, kinship, and totemism, which he analysed as though they were language systems. He believed that the structures he identified corresponded to structures inherent in the human mind.

The elements making up a literary work were held to have no intrinsic significance; their importance came from the relationships between them, such as parallelism, opposition, and so on. Literary structuralism was analytical rather than evaluative, regarding 'the content' of a narrative as less important than its structure.

2. HUMAN SOCIETY

2.1 Social Relations

Sociology is a branch of the science of human behaviour that seeks to discover the causes and effects that arise in social relations among persons and in the intercommunication and interaction among persons and groups. It includes the study of the customs, structures, and institutions that emerge from interaction, of the forces that hold together and weaken them, and of the effects that participation in groups and organizations have on the behaviour and character of persons. Sociology is also concerned with the basic nature of human society, locally and universally, and with the various processes that preserve continuity and produce change.

It is social life that is distinctive in the regulation of behaviour in human beings; the human animal does not have such instincts as serve to guide the behaviour of lower animals, and he is therefore more dependent on social organization than is any other species. Institutionalized social forms therefore are assumed to play the major part in influencing human actions, and it is the task of sociology to discover how these forms operate on the person, as well as how they are established, develop, elaborate, interact with one another, and decay and disappear.

Among the most important of such structures is the family, the subject of an important field of sociology. The peer group, the community, the economic and political orders, various voluntary associations, and special organizations such as the church and the military are of particular importance in this inquiry.

Though sociology can be considered as a part of the Western tradition of rational inquiry inaugurated by the ancient Greeks, it is specifically the offspring of 18th- and 19th-century philosophy and has been viewed as a reaction against the frequently non-scientific approaches of classical philosophy and folklore to social phenomena. It was for a time presented as a part of moral philosophy, which covered the subject matter that eventually also, became the concern of the various social sciences that are now separate from moral philosophy. Some aspects of other fields remain of interest to the sociologist.

Although psychology has traditionally centred its interest on the individual and his internal mental mechanisms, and although sociology has given its major attention to collective aspects of human behaviour, the two disciplines share the subfield of social psychology. The relation of sociology to social anthropology is even closer, and until about the first quarter of the 20th century the two subjects were usually combined in one department, differentiated mainly by the emphasis of the anthropologists on the sociology of preliterate peoples.

Recently even this distinction has been fading, as social anthropologists have increasingly added studies of various aspects of modern society to their field of interest. Political science and economics had much of their early development in the practical interests of nations and for a time evolved separately from basic sociology; but recently in both fields an awareness of the potential utility of some infusion of sociological concepts and methods has brought relations closer. A somewhat similar situation has also been developing in respect to law, education, and religion and to a lesser extent in such contrasting fields as engineering and architecture.

Nineteenth-century sociology, influenced by the successes of biology and evolutionary theory, took an interest in resemblances between men and lower animals--in their having, for example, similar instincts--and also in the parallels between biological and social evolution. These interests have declined, but sociology continues to share with the other sciences some interest in ecology, behavioural genetics, and questions of fertility and mortality as they relate to population studies. There is also a conviction among sociologists that contact between physiology and sociology is necessary to avoid errors of ignorance in both fields.

2.2 Status of contemporary sociology

The Greek philosophers and the line of European philosophers in the succeeding centuries throughout Western civilization discussed much of the subject matter of sociology without thinking of it as a distinct subject. In the early 19th century all the subject matter of the social sciences was discussed under the heading of moral philosophy. Even after Auguste Comte introduced the word *sociologie* in 1838, the matter was combined with other subjects for some sixty years. Not until the universities undertook a commitment to the subject could a person make a living as a full-time sociologist. This commitment had first to be made by scholars of other fields, of which history was a principal early sponsor.

As early as 1876, at the new Johns Hopkins University, some of the content of sociology was taught in the department of history and politics. In 1889 at the University of Kansas, the word appeared in the title of the department of history and sociology. In 1890 at Colby College, a historian, Albion Small, taught a course called sociology, as did Franklin H. Giddings in the same year at Bryn Mawr College.

But the first real commitment to the creation of a field of sociology took place in 1892 at the new University of Chicago, where newly arrived Albion Small asked for and received permission to create a department called sociology--the first such in the world. In the following year or two, departments in the subject were founded at Columbia, Kansas, and Michigan and very soon afterward at Yale, Brown, and many other universities. By the late 1890s nearly all of the educational institutions in the United States either had departments of sociology or offered courses in the subject.

In 1895 the *American Journal of Sociology* began publication at the University of Chicago, in time to be followed by a large number of journals in many other countries. Ten years later the *American Sociological Society* was organized, also to be followed in time by a large number of national, regional, international, and special sociological organizations. These quickly institutionalized the subject and have continuously served to guide its directions and to establish, very roughly, its boundaries. Eventually in 1949 the International Sociological Association was established under the sponsorship of UNESCO, and Louis Wirth (1897-1952) of the University of Chicago was elected its first president.

The rapid growth in numbers of full-time sociologists, along with growth of publications, allowed the content of the discipline to expand rapidly. By 1970 there were more than a dozen important sociological journals and an indefinite number of minor journals in the U.S., as well as a considerable number in other nations. Research grew throughout the 20th century at an accelerated pace, especially since the 1920s, partly because of strong financial support from foundations, government, commercial sources, and private gifts. Along with this came a flourishing of research institutes, some affiliated with university departments and some independent. A small but increasing number of sociologists gain their livelihood through full-time research independent of universities.

Similar developments have occurred in various other parts of the world, with variations resulting from special conditions in each case. In France, where Auguste Comte and later Émile Durkheim gave early impetus to sociology, there was early development in many fields of the subject. The two world wars slowed the development, but after 1945 a strong revival of interest in sociology took place, during which the French government established a number of institutes in the social sciences at the level of institutes in the natural sciences, including several in Paris for sociological research--notably the Centre d'Études Sociologiques, the Institut National d'Études Démographiques, and the Maison des Sciences de l'Homme. These institutes receive government funds and employ many full-time sociologists, some of them among the prominent scholars in the nation.

French universities have been somewhat more conservative; the Sorbonne, for example, had in 1970 only one chair officially assigned to sociology. The new University of Nanterre, however, established a department with four professorships. A rich amount of research publication has been produced in France since World War II, particularly in general sociology, theory, methodology, social psychology, industrial sociology, and the sociology of work.

German sociology had a strong base in the late 19th century and afterward, and the writings of Ferdinand Tönnies, Max Weber, Georg Simmel, and others were influential in all parts of the world. By the early 1930s, however, official Nazi hostility had impeded its development and by the time of World War II had destroyed it as an academic subject in Germany.

Immediately after the war a new generation of scholars, aided by visiting sociologists, imported the new empirical research methods and began the development of a style of German sociology much different from the earlier theoretical and philosophical traditions. At the University of Frankfurt, Max Horkheimer's Institut für Sozialforschung (social research), established by private financing before the war, was revived and has stimulated much research production. West German universities remained conservative for a time, but two newly created universities--the Free University of Berlin and the University of Constance--made sociology one of their major subjects.

By 1970 most West German universities had at least one chair in sociology. National needs received special emphasis, including administrative research of use to planning, studies of unemployment, youth problems, and delinquency. A significant amount of research also is published in such fields as rural sociology, political sociology, and the family.

In Great Britain, despite the early prominence of Herbert Spencer and L.T. Hobhouse, sociology was little regarded by leading universities until the mid-20th century. Before World War II Britain excelled in anthropology, especially in the study of non-white societies of the empire. Sociology concentrated on studies of the poor, and much of it was undertaken by persons whose affiliation was similar to that of social workers in the United States.

The major pre-war sociology department, at the London School of Economics, had the objective more of social reform than scientific research. In the post-war period, however, a considerable revival of sociology took place; Oxford and Cambridge recognized the subject by creating positions for sociologists, and various new universities established chairs and departments. Significant work in Britain has been done in such fields as population and demography, sociology of organization, and general sociology. The Tavistock Institute of Human Relations in London has become world famous and concentrates on human relations in the family, the work group, and organizations.

A parallel growth took place in Canada, Australia, and New Zealand. Canada, with some apparent reluctance, allowed itself to be much influenced by American sociology and has built many new departments with sociologists trained in the United States.

The Scandinavian countries have also to a considerable extent adopted the methods and some of the content of American sociology, and the subject has had rapid development in many of the universities and in research institutes, some of which are connected with universities. There is also a considerable amount of interchange between sociologists in these countries.

Japan has a record of much sociological activity dating back to the 1870s. The Japanese Sociological Society (Nippon Shakai Gakkai), headquartered at the University of Tokyo, was founded in 1923; by 1960 there were about 150 universities and colleges with courses in the subject. In the early period sociology was nearly all imported; Comte and Spencer, and later Giddings and Gabriel Tarde, were their important theorists. After World War II there were rapid changes in sociology in Japan, with empirical research methods largely replacing the earlier philosophical style. Importations from American sociology became abundant. Popular among these were industrial sociology, educational sociology, public opinion research, and the study of mass communications.

Sociology in the former Soviet Union was long held back by the perceived incompatibility of the subject with Marxist theory. Eventually, however, it was permitted to develop, and sociological institutes and chairs of sociology increased. By 1970 the Soviet Sociological Association had more than a thousand members. Leading research interests included such subjects as labour productivity, education, crime, and alcoholism. Soviet sociology generally displayed an apparent tendency to avoid issues that might have implied conflict with Marxist thought.

Nations under the influence of the Soviet Union were also from time to time inhospitable to sociology, but the strong interest of younger scholars made possible some relaxation of this opposition, and in the second half of the 20th century there was considerable progress of sociology in such countries as Hungary, Poland, the Czech Republic, and Slovakia, with occasional setbacks in some areas.

In Israel the dominant department of sociology is at the Hebrew University in Jerusalem, where there are also several research institutes. Israeli sociology maintains continuous close contacts with American sociology and many of the leading Israeli sociologists have had training or teaching experience in the United States. Among the specialties in Israel are research in methodology, communication, criminology, and the collective settlements (*kibbutzim*) in which new forms of custom and social organization are observed while under development.

The passing of the Fascist regime in Italy and the relative liberalization in Spain opened the door to sociology, and academic chairs and research institutes are gradually increasing in these countries. Of particular interest are studies of industrial efficiency and social mobility. The general conservatism of universities, however, may constitute a retarding influence for some time to come.

In Latin America objective sociology has been much resisted, partly because it has been viewed as a threat to the political and social order but also because of meagre financial support of research and the low salary level of professors, many of whom must supplement their earnings in the practice of law, in civil service, and in other occupations. In the 1960s, however, the number of full-time chairs increased, and a number of research institutes, some financed by U.S. funds, were established. Political instability in some countries remains a major hindrance, and in such countries able scholars continue to be forced from their university positions from time to time.

Little by little, sociology is penetrating into some of the developing nations. A number of African universities have formed departments, and the subject is gaining in importance in the Philippines, India, Indonesia, and Pakistan.

2.3 Sociology comes into being

Sociology came into being in precisely these terms, and during much of the century it was not easy to distinguish between a great deal of so-called sociology and social or cultural anthropology. Even if almost no sociologists in the century made empirical studies of primitive peoples, as did the anthropologists, their interest in the origin, development, and probable future of mankind was not less great than what could be found in the writings of the anthropologists.

It was Auguste Comte who coined the word sociology, and he used it to refer to what he imagined would be a single, all-encompassing, science of society that would take its place at the top of the hierarchy of sciences--a hierarchy that Comte saw as including astronomy (the oldest of the sciences historically) at the bottom and with physics, chemistry, and biology rising in that order to sociology, the latest and grandest of the sciences.

There was no thought in Comte's mind--nor was there in the mind of Herbert Spencer, whose general view of sociology was very much like Comte's--of there being other, competing social sciences. Sociology would be to the whole of the social world what each of the other great sciences was to its appropriate sphere of reality.

Both Comte and Spencer believed that civilization as a whole was the proper subject of sociology. Their works were concerned, for the most part, with describing the origins and development of civilization and also of each of its major institutions. Both declared sociology's main divisions to be "statics" and "dynamics," the former concerned with processes of order in society, the latter with processes of evolutionary change in society. Both men also saw all existing societies in the world as reflective of the successive stages through which Western society had advanced in time over a period of tens of thousands of years.

Not all sociologists in the 19th century conceived their discipline in this light, however. Side by side with the "grand" view represented by Comte and Spencer were those in the century who were primarily interested in the social problems that they saw around them--consequences, as they interpreted them, of the two revolutions, the industrial and democratic. Thus in France just after midcentury, Frédéric Le Play published a monumental study of the social aspects of the working classes in Europe, *Les Ouvriers européens*, which compared families and communities in all parts of Europe and even other parts of the world.

Alexis de Tocqueville, especially in the second volume of his *Democracy in America* (1835), provided an account of the customs, social structures, and institutions in America, dealing with these--and also with the social and psychological problems of Americans in that day--as aspects of the impact of the democratic and industrial revolutions upon traditional society.

At the very end of the 19th century, in both France and Germany, there appeared some of the works in sociology that were to prove most lasting in their effects upon 20th-century sociology. Ferdinand Tönnies, in his *Gemeinschaft und Gesellschaft* (1887; translated as *Community and Society*), sought to explain all major social problems in the West as the consequence of the West's historical transition from the communal, status-based, concentric society of the Middle Ages to the more individualistic, impersonal, and large-scale society of the democratic-industrial period.

In general terms, allowing for individual variations of theme, these were the views of Max Weber, Georg Simmel, and Émile Durkheim (all of whom also wrote in the late 19th and early 20th century). These were the men who, starting from the problems of Western society that could be traced to the effects of the two revolutions, did the most to establish the discipline of sociology as it is found for the most part in the 20th century.

2.4 National methodological preferences

All the methods described above are widely used, but their relative popularity in various nations is somewhat related to both the nature of the financial support of research, and the field of national interest.

Where agricultural problems are of major interest, rural sociology and community studies that can be conducted inexpensively by one or a few investigators are popular. In France, Italy, and several other European nations, industrial sociology is understandably important, much of it based on case studies of industries and the experiences of workers. Sociology in Great Britain, the Scandinavian countries, and Japan covers most of the fields mentioned above.

The broad methodological concepts have varied somewhat according to the country and according to the subfield of sociology. Early in the century there was presumed to be a general difference between the sociologies of European countries and the sociologies of the United States--the former appearing to prefer broad sociological theory based on philosophical methods and the latter showing more inclination toward induction and empiricism. Such differences have declined steadily in recent times, and what differences remain may be in part a result of the differential financing of expensive research.

In the former U.S.S.R. and in nations that were under its influence there was much emphasis on the concepts and methods of Marxist sociology, which had only a small following elsewhere. A more important methodological issue divides basic scientific sociology from applied sociology; scholars interested in applied sociology tend to deprecate the methods and findings of the scientific sociologists as being either irrelevant or supportive of an objectionable status quo. Issues of ethics have also in recent years been raised, particularly in regard to observations and experiments in which the privacy of subjects may be felt to be invaded.

2.5 Emerging subfields

Because human behaviour observes no limits in its directions, it is possible for sociologists to extend their inquiries accordingly. The expansion of sociological interests thus has involved some penetration of adjacent traditional academic fields, such as political science, economics, anthropology, psychology, communications, speech, and to some extent even physiology and zoology. Fields within traditional sociology have also broadened their content, producing such expanded subjects as ecology and comparative sociology. Not all this extension is new, however, since much of the 19th century sociology was also very broad, especially the cosmic sociology of one worker, Lester F. Ward, who conceived sociology as the science of sciences, properly covering and organizing all knowledge.

Applications of sociology also appear to be spreading in a variety of directions, and here the possibilities seem unlimited. Sociologists aid industries in obtaining more efficient production; they help unions to increase their power; they organize rebellions of young persons, reform disorganized villages, counsel persons and families, and gives or sell services to a wide variety of consumers. To what extent these applied activities will continue to spread will doubtless depend on their effectiveness relative to other means of gaining the same effects.

There is also an expansion of sociology into other than practical applications; for example, there is mathematical sociology, in which mathematical models of social behaviour are developed without systematic observations of behaviour. These efforts are not directed toward immediate human use, but may have value as bases for comparison with real behaviour and thus aid explanation of behavioural causes. A mathematical model of a completely just theoretical process of social mobility, for example, could be useful as a standard for comparing actual mobility at different times and in different nations.

3. HISTORICAL DEVELOPMENT OF SOCIOLOGY

3.1 Social Darwinism and evolutionism

The founders of sociology spent decades almost exclusively in the process of finding a direction for their new discipline. In the course of this groping effort they tried several highly divergent pathways, some suggested by methods and contents of other sciences, others invented outright by the imagination of the scholar.

Darwinian evolutionary theory doubtlessly suggested a way in which a science of human behaviour could become academically respectable, and a line of creative thinkers, including Herbert Spencer, Benjamin Kidd, Lewis H. Morgan, E.B. Tylor, L.T. Hobhouse, and others, developed analogies between human society and the biological organism and introduced into sociological theory such biological concepts as variation, natural selection, and inheritance--evolutionary factors resulting in the progress of societies through stages of savagery and barbarism to civilization, by virtue of the survival of the fittest.

Some writers also perceived in the growth stages of each individual a recapitulation of these stages of society. Strange customs were thus accounted for on the assumption that they were throwbacks to an earlier useful practice; an example offered was the make-believe struggle sometimes enacted at marriage ceremonies between the bridegroom and the relatives of the bride, reflecting an earlier bride-capture custom.

Social Darwinism waned in the 20th century, but in its popular period it was used to justify unrestricted competition and a laissez-faire doctrine in order that the "fittest" would survive and that civilization would continue to advance.

3.2 Ward, Lester Frank

(Born June 18, 1841, Joliet, Ill., U.S., died April 18, 1913, Washington, D.C.)

Ward was instrumental in establishing sociology as an academic discipline in the United States. An optimist who believed that the social sciences had already given mankind the information basic to happiness, he advocated a planned, or "telic," society ("sociocracy") in which education, nationally organized, would be the dynamic factor. Social scientists, assembled into a legislative advisory academy in Washington, D.C., would occupy in his system much the same role as did the sociologist-priests in the utopian plan of the French sociologist Auguste Comte.

After fighting for the Union in the American Civil War, he obtained degrees in botany and law. For most of his life he worked for the federal government, mainly in the fields of geology, paleontology, botany, and paleobotany; he made some significant contributions to botanical theory. In 1906, when he was 65 years old, he was appointed professor of sociology at Brown University, Providence, R.I.

Ward followed Comte in conceiving of sociology as the fundamental social science, the primary responsibility of which is to teach methods of achieving a better society. Ward's emphasis on social function and planning, rather than social structure, had considerable effect on Thorstein Veblen and the institutional economists.

The original subject of Ward's most important book, *Dynamic Sociology*, 2 vol. (1883), was education. By 1876 Ward had shifted the focus of the work, which was begun in 1869, to sociology. Among his other writings are *Pure Sociology* (1903), *A Textbook of Sociology* (with James Quayle Dealey, 1905), and *Applied Sociology* (1906), which concerns his ideas of "social telesis," sociocracy, and social planning.

3.3 Methodology in contemporary sociology

Much of 19th-century sociology was devoid of systematic method, but late in the period the proliferation of schools of thought, based on speculative sociologies, made evident the need for ways of obtaining verifiable knowledge. Early attempts were crude and unfruitful; such broad surveyors as Charles Booth, who produced a monumental series on London, relied mainly on the gathering of masses of facts. Frédéric Le Play in France made extensive studies of family budgets. Herbert Spencer and others assembled vast stores of observations made by other persons, using these to illustrate and support generalizations already formulated.

Early exploitation of statistical materials, such as officially recorded rates of births, deaths, crimes, and suicides, provided only a moderate advance in knowledge, because this approach was too capable of supporting preconceived ideas. Among the most successful of this type of study was research on suicide by Émile Durkheim, whose successors in France and elsewhere developed the methodology a considerable way toward scientific adequacy.

After the turn of the century, interest in, and the determination to achieve, a sociological methodology grew steadily. The *Methodological Note*, constituting the greater part of a volume in W.I. Thomas and Florian Znaniecki's *Polish Peasant in Europe and America* (5 vol., 1918-20), has been recognized as an important advance, not so much in methodology as in committing sociologists to the task of achieving it.

Significant advances toward scientific effectiveness occurred at the University of Chicago in the 1920s. Under the stimulation of Robert E.

Park, Burgess, and their colleagues a series of studies of the metropolis was conducted. The spirit was inductive, and hypotheses were discovered in rather than imposed on gathered information. Large numbers of students took part in the effort and contributed to both methods and findings.

A conspicuous part of the effort consisted of mapping locations of various phenomena: land uses, residences of population categories (racial, ethnic, and occupational), residences of persons who commit various types of crimes or suicide, families becoming divorced or broken through desertion, and so forth. But along with such information on spatial distributions, data were sought by other means, including participant observation in groups and communities, gathering of life histories and case studies, assembly of relevant historical information, study of the life cycles of social movements and sects, and the like.

Attention was explicitly given to the improvement of methodology in all of these efforts, to an extent approximately equal to the attention given to substantive findings. Here for the first time was developed a large-scale cooperative effort in which theory, methodology, and findings evolved together in an inductive process. The influence of this development at Chicago spread rapidly about the United States and in time influenced sociology almost everywhere it was studied in the world.

3.4 Statistics in sociology

Statistical methods were introduced into sociology from other sciences, and virtually from the start, sociologists have found statistical measures of relationship of great value. Karl Pearson's "coefficient of correlation," for example, has been a popular as well as important statistical concept for the measurement of cause-and-effect relationships among continuous variables.

This method reveals the *degree* of causal connection between two variables, though not necessarily the *nature* of the connection. In sociology there are types of data that are relevant to causal inquiry but do not have the characteristics that qualify for the Pearsonian coefficient. Thus, much development work has been done to provide other measures of association involving, for example, rankings of groups or individuals or qualitative comparisons (such as whether males and females differ systematically in specified qualities).

Factor analysis, also based on an elaboration of Pearsonian correlation, performs another valuable service to sociology. If there are a large number of variables causally intertwined in a complex way, it is possible that these variables can be reduced to a small number of factors. Fifty different tests of mental ability, for instance, may be in fact 50 different mixtures of only seven or eight dimensions of mental ability.

Factor analysis involves reducing such variables to a more limited number of common factors and determining the relative importance of each factor in the original variables. The process has its imperfections and the computations are laborious, but the availability of computers has overcome the latter disadvantage, and in recent years the technique has increased in use.

These statistical methods and many others are applicable to all branches of sociology and are increasingly fruitful in transforming sociology into science. In general, the growth of statistical methods has been so rapid that the invention of new techniques has outstripped the ability of scholars to find data worthy of the devices. Thus the rate of progress in the near future may depend to a large extent on improvement in satisfactory data gathering and measurement.

Methodologies of data gathering are in fact of major interest in sociology. Techniques of observation--of persons, groups, organizations, communities--have been extensively developed. Important for the same purpose are the various means of quantifying these observations, including scales of various kinds, sociometric techniques that make interrelations subject to statistical analysis, content analysis of written materials, and classification of cross-cultural information.

3.5 Other sociological studies

An extensive literature on religious sects and similar groups has also developed. To some extent this has been influenced by the German theologian Ernst Troeltsch in his distinction between church and sect (see below Theological studies). Notable among modern investigators of sectarianism is the British scholar Bryan Wilson. Church organizations also have attempted to use the insights of sociology in the work of evangelism and other church-related activities--a use of the discipline that is sometimes called "religious sociology" to distinguish it from the more theoretical and "objective" sociology of religion.

Coordination between sociology and the history of religions is not usually very close, since the two disciplines operate as separate departments in most universities and often in different faculties. From the sociological end, Weber represents one kind of synthesis; from the history-of-religions end, the writings of the German-American scholar Joachim Wach (see below The "Chicago school") were quite influential. In his book *Sociology of Religion* he attempted to exhibit the ways in which the community institutions of religion express certain attitudes and experiences. This view was in accordance with his insistence on the practical and existential side of religion, over against the intellectualist tendency to treat the correlate of the group as being a system of beliefs.

Among the more recent theorists of the sociology of religion is the influential and eclectic American scholar Peter Berger. In *The Sacred Canopy* he draws on elements from Marx, Durkheim, Weber, and others, creating a lively theoretical synthesis. One problem is raised by his method, however; he espouses what he calls "methodological atheism" in his work, which appears to presuppose a view about religion.

Despite Berger's sympathy in dealing with religious phenomena, the methodological stance adopted in this book seems to imply a reductionist position--namely, one in which religious beliefs are explained by reference to basically nonreligious sentiments, socio-psychological circumstances, and other factors. In itself, this is a theory having possibilities, for the study of religion cannot rule out a priori the thesis that religion is a projection--*e.g.,* that it rests upon an illusion--or other such theses; but the question arises as to whether or not the methods espoused in the scientific study of religion have already secretly prejudged the issue.

On the whole, modern sociology is largely geared to dealing with Western religious institutions and practices, though some notable work has been done, especially since World War II, in Asian sociology of religion. Emphasis has been placed upon the process of secularization in a number of Western sociological studies (which have had some impact on the formation of modern Christian theology), notably in *The Secular City* of the American theologian Harvey Cox. There are indications that the process of secularization does not occur in the same degree or occurs in a different manner in non-Western cultures.

In general, the main question of the sociology of religion concerns the effectiveness with which it can relate to other studies of religion. This question is posed in *The Scientific Study of Religion*, by the American sociologist J. Milton Yinger. A similar tendency is noted in the synthesis between the history and the sociology of religion in a new-style evolutionism propounded by another American scholar, Robert Bellah.

3.6 Sociology of knowledge

The use of the word *ideology* in the pejorative sense of false consciousness is found not only in the writings of Marx himself but in those of other exponents of what has come to be known as the sociology of knowledge, including the German sociologists Max Weber and Karl Mannheim, and numerous lesser figures. Few such writers are wholly consistent in their use of the term, but what is characteristic of their approach is their method of regarding idea systems as the outcome or expression of certain interests. In calling such idea systems ideologies, they are treating them as things whose true nature is concealed; they consider the task of sociological research to be the unveiling of what Mannheim called the "life conditions which produce ideologies."

From this perspective, the economic science of Adam Smith, for example, is not to be understood as an independent intellectual construction or to be judged in terms of its truth, consistency, or clarity; rather, it is to be seen as the expression of bourgeois interests, as part of the ideology of capitalism.

The sociology of knowledge in its more recent formulations has sought support in Freudian psychology (notably in borrowing from Freud the concepts of the unconscious and of rationalization), in order to suggest that ideologies are the unconscious rationalizations of class interests.

This refinement has enabled sociologists of knowledge to rid their theory of the disagreeable and unscientific element of bald accusation; they no longer have to brand Adam Smith as a deliberate champion of the bourgeois ethos but can see him now as simply the unconscious spokesman of capitalism. At the same time, these sociologists of knowledge have argued that Freudian psychology is itself no less a form of ideology than is Adam Smith's economics, for Freud's method of psychoanalysis is essentially a technique for adjusting rebellious minds to the demands and constraints of bourgeois society.

Critics of the sociology of knowledge have argued that if all philosophy is ideology, then the sociology of knowledge must itself be an ideology like any other idea system and equally devoid of independent validity; that if all seeming truth is veiled rationalization of interest, then the sociology of knowledge cannot be true.

It has been suggested that although Weber and Mannheim inspired most of the work that has been done by sociologists of knowledge their own writings may perhaps be exempted from this criticism, if only on the ground that neither of them put forward a consistent or unambiguous theory of ideology.

Both used the word *ideology* in different ways at different times. Weber was in part concerned to reverse Marx's theory that all idea systems are products of economic structures, by demonstrating conversely that some economic structures are the product of idea systems (that Protestantism, for example, generated capitalism and not capitalism Protestantism). Mannheim, on the other hand, tried to restore in a more elaborate form Marx's suggestion that ideologies are the product of the social structure.

But Mannheim's analysis may have been obscured by his proposal that the word *ideology* should be reserved for idea systems that are more or less conservative, and the word *utopia* for idea systems of a more revolutionary or millenarian nature. Mannheim did not, however, remain faithful to this stipulative definition, even in his book entitled *Ideology and Utopia*.

On the other hand, Mannheim was well aware of the implication of the doctrine that all idea systems have a class basis and a class bias. As a way out of the dilemma he envisaged the possibility of a classless class of intellectuals, a "socially unattached intelligentsia," as he put it, capable of thinking independently by virtue of its independence from any class interest or affiliation. Such a detached group might hope to acquire knowledge that was *not* ideology. This vision of a small elite of superior minds rising above the myths of ordinary society seemed to some readers to put Mannheim closer to Plato than to Marx and to cast new doubts on the claim of the sociology of knowledge to be a science.

3.7 Findings of sociology

The ideas and images of a religion are much influenced by the social culture in which it emerges. Some of the oldest social institutions and practices, such as those concerning birth and death, marriage and the family, and art and music, have developed in a religious context. Religion has often been a driving force in the reform of social abuses, but also it has been associated with reaction and oppression.

More recently, the sociology of religion--influenced by contemporary sociology--has been concerned with making use of sociological criteria and of demographical and statistical studies in planning the church's mission and appraising its significance.

3.8 Findings of religious history

Conclusions in the history of religions have been largely determined by the particular ideas of man or history with which the study was approached. Some scholars have supposed that at the dawn of human existence there was a belief in a single god and that only later there occurred a development into a belief in many gods as well as animism (a belief in souls or spirits in man and other aspects of nature).

Other scholars have supposed an evolutionary development of religion, which only reached monotheism--considered to be the highest form of religious belief--after a long period of purification. The two approaches sponsor, respectively, two contrasting myths about primitive man. According to the one, there was once a golden age of innocence and harmony; according to the other, the life of the earliest man was nasty, brutish, and short.

Granted the ubiquity of religion and its diversity, historians have found no universal essence expressible in terms of common beliefs. What is probably common to all religions is nothing more than the claim that reality is not restricted solely to what is yielded by sense experience itself.

3.9 Scientific status

It is evident that sociology has not achieved triumphs comparable to those of the several older and more heavily supported sciences. A variety of interpretations have been offered to explain the difference--most frequently, that the growth of knowledge in the science of sociology is more random than cumulative. The true situation appears to be that in some parts of the discipline--such as methodology, ecology, demography, the study of social differentiation and mobility, attitude research, and the study of small-group interaction processes, public opinion, and mass communication--there has in fact taken place a slow but accelerating accumulation of organized and tested knowledge.

In some other fields the expansion of the volume of literature has not appeared to have had this property. Critics have attributed the slow pace to a variety of factors--the appetite of sociologists for neologisms and jargon, a disposition for pseudo-quantification, and excessive concern with imitation of the methods of natural sciences, overdependence on data from interviews, questionnaires, and informal observations. All these shortcomings can be found in contemporary sociology, but none is characteristic of all areas.

In general there has been progress toward efficient terminology and methods and toward more satisfactory data, and conclusions are increasingly based on the harmonious mixture of research methods applied to varied and repeated studies, and therefore are less dependent on the strength of one particular methodological device.

Bias, in more than one direction, is sometimes presumed to be a chronic affliction of sociology. This may arise in part from the fact that the subject matter of sociology is familiar and important in the daily life of everyone, so that there exist many opportunities for the abundant variations in philosophical outlook and individual preferences to appear as irrational bias.

Thus critics have expressed disapproval of the sociologists' scepticism on various matters of faith, of their amoral relativism concerning customs, of their apparent oversimplifications of some principles, and of their particular fashions in categorization and abstraction. But scepticism toward much of the content of folk knowledge is a characteristic of all science, and relativism can be interpreted as merely an avoidance of antiscientific ethnocentrism. Furthermore, abstraction, categorization, and simplification are necessary to the advancement of knowledge, and no one system satisfies everyone.

The dispute about the main purpose of sociology, whether it works to understand behaviour, or to cause social change, is a dispute found in every pursuit of scientific knowledge, and such polarization is far from absolute. Persons differ in the degree to which they regard the value of science as an intellectual understanding of the cosmos or as an instrument for immediate improvement of the human lot.

Since even the "purest" scientist conceives of his work as benefiting mankind, the issue narrows to a difference in preference between an *ad hoc* attack on immediate human problems and a long-run trust that basic knowledge, gathered without reference to present urgencies, is even more valuable.

Sociologists differ on this issue; in some countries there is much pressure toward early practicality of results; in others, including the United States, the larger number of scholars and the principal sociological associations have shown preference for "basic science." In very recent times, however, there has emerged a radical movement among students in various countries involving advocacy of complete commitment to action on current political and social problems.

A degree of polarization has also arisen over the proper strategy for research--whether research should take its directions from the needs of society and mankind or from the evolving theoretical corpus of sociology. In nations that allow academic freedom such disputes are usually of low intensity, because each scholar selects his research interests on any basis he prefers, including that of personal taste. In this way presumably the motivation of the investigator is maximized.

Sociologists most interested in action express impatience at the claims of others who prefer to separate their research from personal values. Much of the dispute prevails only because the two sides argue past each other. There can be wide agreement that no human being is without personal values, that research forced to confirm a particular set of values is not good science, and that there can be scientific issues toward which a particular investigator is value-neutral.

In research that is susceptible to contamination by the values of the worker, it is generally possible to minimize the damage by employing methodological devices that help to insulate the scientist from his wishes for a particular outcome--such devices as objective observational techniques and measurement methods, independent and blind analysis of results, and so forth.

4. SOCIOLOGICAL KNOWLEDGE

4.1 Problems of bias

Since most sociological knowledge is based on the study of samples from some larger universe of items, the possibilities of major errors from sampling bias constitute a methodological issue. Where biases cannot be controlled, the direction and extent may sometimes be estimated, but elimination of biases through use of quotas--or, when possible, random methods--yields the best results. This can be done, for example, by first randomly selecting a number of definable regions and metropolitan areas, then selecting randomly from each such area certain urban blocks and rural segments, then further selecting from these segments certain dwelling units, and finally selecting from the dwelling units the specific persons to constitute the sample.

In every stage of the process of discovery in sociology there are possibilities of error, and recognition of these is a part of the progress of sociological methodology. There is continuous creation of technical devices to reduce such errors and to estimate the amount of error that has not been eliminated.

4.2 Emerging methodologies

After the easiest sociological questions have been answered, the further progress of research requires ever greater effort and cost, and the proportion of discoveries by individual investigators declines as the necessity for larger teamwork research expands. This foreshadows increasing complexity of the organization of research, as has already taken place in older sciences. Large-scale research in sociology is made possible, and perhaps inevitable, by the availability of expensive computers, elaborate techniques of multivariate analysis, and the storage of information in the form of data banks and the like.

The strongest methodological emphasis in the near future is likely to be on the processes of rigorous testing of generalizations that now appear to be of strategic value in the general structure of sociological knowledge. Complete surprises in the field of human behaviour are less likely than in other sciences, since most of the possible human situations have been familiar in folk knowledge as well as in academic sociology. But the subject contains many inconsistent principles, and few of these have been put to a definitive test, partly from lack of adequate methodology and to some extent from shortage of funds and scientific manpower.

4.3 Experiments

Experimental methods, once believed to be inapplicable to sociological research, were extensively applied by psychologists, first on individuals and later on groups. By the 1930s some psychologists--notably Kurt Lewin and his colleagues and also Muzafer Sherif--found means of conducting experiments on social interaction. Sociologists soon followed their example and in time a number of laboratories for such research were established; Robert F. Bales, at Harvard, has made systematic observations on interaction in small, artificial groups and has produced clear and useful results, confirmed in other laboratories.

Experiments are also conducted in classrooms, in summer camps, in formal organizations, and elsewhere. In general the success of experimentation has been greatest in simple situations in which the number of variables is limited. Complex experiments, however, are possible in some circumstances, and the design of complex formal experiments is becoming a developed art in a variety of fields, including sociology.

4.4 Ecological patterning

Ecological methods in sociology were first developed in connection with research on the characteristics of the metropolis, especially in regard to features of a non-social character, such as the patterns resulting from the distribution and movements of populations and institutions in the general process of struggling for advantage. A conspicuous part of most early urban studies consisted of mapping such distributions.

The patterns of land values, of locations of various types of businesses and industries, of ethnic categories of the population, and of types of behaviour (delinquency and crime, vice, family disorganization, mental disorders, etc.) were all shown to be interrelated in a general urban ecology. This fact was then shown to be related to many aspects of behaviour of city people, and valuable contributions were made to such general sociological topics as social differentiation, migration and vertical mobility, and social disorganization.

In recent years sociological ecology has broadened in meaning and in the elaboration of methods. One modern approach, known as ecosystem theory, consists of tracing general patterns of flow of materials, energy, and information into a system and their transformation during the flow through the system, among other things.

4.5 Emerging roles for sociologists

In general the principal employment of sociologists has been in educational institutions, but recently, in various countries, there has been an increasing penetration into other fields of activity. Sociologists, particularly in earlier decades, have been involved in various organized agencies devoted to social work. They also have participated in government work at various levels, from the lower bureaucratic ranks all the way to high administrative responsibility, and in the case of Thomás Masaryk, former president of Czechoslovakia, to the highest office of a nation. In the United States sociologists have been extensively employed in the Bureau of the Census; the Bureau of the Budget; the Institutes of Health; various other sections of the Department of Health, Education, and Welfare; and the office of the president, where they have made contributions to policy.

Other directions of sociological activity include the roles of consultant, social critic, social activist, and even revolutionary. When the activity diverges far enough from traditional academic sociology, it may cease to be regarded as sociological, but it appears likely that sociologists will continue to spread their activities over the ever-widening region of national or global concern, in the name of their science or otherwise.

4.6 Determinism

In this case determinism refers to economy, environment, and biology. Except in the philosophy of Karl Marx (whose writings ranged over all the social science fields rather than specifically in sociology), the doctrine of economic determinism never gained a strong foothold in sociology. This was not a consequence of scholarly ignorance; sociologists of all periods have read Marx and have usually read such writers as the historian Charles A. Beard, who emphasized economic self-interest, and Werner Sombart, the German sociologist who had been a convinced Marxist in his early career. But there have been only some adapted reflections of these economic views in the writings of such sociologists as Franklin H. Giddings or Frank H. Hankins who viewed some political and religious doctrines as rationalizations of economic and social interests.

The human geographers--Ellsworth Huntington, Ellen Semple, Friedrich Ratzel, Paul Vidal de La Blache, Jean Brunhes, and others--were also read critically by sociologists but did not make a lasting major contribution to the mainstream of sociological thought, even though there are some who believe that the social morphology of Émile Durkheim, Maurice Halbwachs, and others--that is, their theories about the roles of individuals interacting in a social system--grew in part from this interest.

Aside from the interest in evolution, organismic analogies, and the instinct concept, sociologists have not found biological determination of value to them and have spent more energy in refuting it than in making use of it.

4.7 Symbolic interactionism

Sociologists did not for long find the 19th-century instinctivist psychology congenial, and most of them also failed to appreciate the doctrines of classical or Watsonian behaviourism, which sought to be totally objective and experimental. One influential movement in social psychology, however, did take early root and eventually became the largest and most influential field in modern American sociology. In recent years it has become known as "symbolic interactionism," but it was under development for decades before it acquired a name.

Out of early ideas expressed by J. Mark Baldwin and William James, a group of three scholars, John Dewey, George H. Mead, and Charles H. Cooley, built the foundations of a psychology that was to become most useful to sociology. In brief, their contribution was to advance the theory that mind and self are not part of the innate equipment of the human organism but arise in experience and are constructed in a social process-- that is, in a process of interaction among persons in intimate, personal communication with one another.

The self, or self-concept, as developed by Mead and others, is thus essentially an internalization of aspects of an interpersonal or social process. It exists in imagery and symbolization and is internalized and organized for each person out of his perception of how other persons conceive him. This self-concept, however inexact, fluctuating, and uncertain, nevertheless functions as a guide in social behaviour--that is, persons tend to act in order to preserve the existing or desired image of their self.

William I. Thomas, a sociologist and colleague of the philosopher Mead at the University of Chicago in the early years of the 20th century, regularly taught a course in social psychology based on Mead's conceptions. Thomas was succeeded in 1919 by Ellsworth Faris, himself a psychologist but later a member of the department of sociology, and through his work the tradition was further developed and brought into closer relation to the sociological tradition of Robert E. Park and Ernest W. Burgess, also at Chicago.

In this tradition an interest in an appropriate methodology accompanied the growth of substantive knowledge; Thomas particularly emphasized the value of extensive use of personal documents, life histories, and autobiographies. In recent years interest in research on the self and self-conscious behaviour has spread widely, and is now participated in by psychologists, philosophers, and essayists, as well as by a movement within sociology called "ethnomethodology," which investigates areas of symbolic interaction by informal observation, reflection, and skilled interpretation, methods sometimes called *Verstehen* (understanding).

4.8 Early functionalism

Following the achievement of a consensus that there should be a place for a science of sociology, there emerged an international effort to define the distinctive character of the subject and especially to clarify its differences from psychology and biology, fields that had also begun to generalize about human behaviour. A Frenchman, Émile Durkheim (1858-1917), was prominent among scholars who considered this question; he argued that there can arise from various kinds of interaction among individuals certain new properties (*sui generis*) not found in separate individuals.

These "social facts" as he called them--collective sentiments, customs, institutions, nations--call for study and explanation on a distinctly sociological level rather than on the level of individual psychology. Furthermore, the interrelations of the parts of a society were perceived as cohering into a unity, an integrated system with a life character of its own, exterior to the individual, and exercising constraint over his behaviour. This direction of causation, from group to individual (rather than the reverse as conceived by most biologists of the time) gave encouragement to the scholar of the new science. Some writers have designated such a view "functionalism," although the term has in recent years acquired some broader variations of meaning.

Durkheim also pointed out that groups could be held together on two contrasting bases: the sentimental attraction of similarities (mechanical solidarity), such as occurs in friendship groups and among relatives and neighbours, and the organization of complementary differences (organic solidarity), such as occurs in industrial, military, governmental, and other organizations that exist because they have tasks to perform. Other theorists of Durkheim's period, notably Henry Maine and Ferdinand Tönnies, made similar distinctions in different terms--*status* and *contract* (Maine) and *Gemeinschaft* and *Gesellschaft* (Tönnies)--and conceived of the major trend of civilization as an expansion of the latter and a relative decline of the former.

Some later anthropologists, especially Bronislaw Malinowski and A.R. Radcliffe-Brown, developed a doctrine also called functionalism, based on the recognition of the interrelatedness of the parts of a society, in bonds so thoroughly interpenetrating that a change in any single element would tend to produce a general disturbance in the whole. This concept gained a following for a time among many social anthropologists, leading some to advocate a policy of complete non-interference with even the most objectionable practices in a preliterate society (such as headhunting) for fear that control might produce far-reaching disorganization.

31

William G. Sumner, in his *Folkways*, defined an institution as a "concept and a structure," meaning a purpose or function that is carried out by some systematic organization of persons. Much of the sociology of Max Weber consists of the analysis of societies in such terms. Georg Simmel, sometimes called the founder of the "formal school" of sociology, viewed society as a process ("something functional") that is real and not merely an abstraction, and he built on this idea a statement of sociology consisting of a systematic analysis of social forms.

4.9 Current trends

It would appear that the growth of sociology will accelerate in the visible future. Among present trends suggesting this likelihood are the increase in public appreciation of the subject, the expansion of available funds for both teaching and research, the steady reduction of sectarian opposition to inquiry into social institutions, the improvement in research methods and methods for gathering data that qualify for modern statistical treatment, and the growth of acceptance and support from scientists in other fields. There are possible factors that could inhibit such growth, such as some forms of extreme nationalism and internal conflict, but such conditions so far have impeded development only locally and temporarily.

Furthermore, it appears likely that public interest in the development of sociological knowledge will increase as a consequence of rising awareness of its promise for human safety and welfare. As the expansion of civilization, with its advanced science and technology, progressively conquers the natural hazards that afflict preliterate and pre-industrial peoples and diminishes such threats as natural catastrophes, famine, and disease, a wide range of new problems emerges.

These are not the menaces of an impersonal nature, but dangers that arise from imperfection in human behaviour, particularly in organized human relations. Wars have shown a tendency to become larger and ever more destructive, and the causes, though far from being understood, clearly lie, in large measure, in the complexities of social organization, in the interaction of great corporate national bodies. There appears to be little hope that politics, unaided by social science among other disciplines, could reverse this trend.

Domestic problems within nations, regions, cities, and towns appear also to become increasing sources of human troubles. There is a general rise in the severity of ethnic hostilities, and of internal conflicts between generations, political factions, and other divisions of the populations. There are also threats to human welfare from various forms of general social disorganization, reflected in the spread of pockets of poverty, crime, vice, political corruption, and family disorganization.

In recent times the threats of overpopulation and potential destruction of the ecological environment have added a further reason for public alarm. Contemporary sociology obviously does not yet provide the solutions, but what prospects of human survival there are depend a great deal on the increase of the applicable knowledge of various social sciences, including sociology.

4.10 Modern determinism

Economic determinism reflects the interest that a few early sociologists took in views of Karl Marx, such as the idea that differentiation into social classes and conflict between these classes derive from economic factors and the belief that the political system is in large part a product of such social stratification.

A residue of this kind of determinism is found among the self-proclaimed "Marxian sociologists." Perhaps the most widely read of these was C. Wright Mills, whose concept of a "power elite" has been extensively and critically examined, with varying resulting judgments on its utility. As Mills saw it, this elite constitutes an integrated ruling group of a capitalistic economic and military system, sometimes called the military-industrial complex, exercising arbitrary power in its own interests. This particular determinism is not supported by most existing objective research, which generally finds a far more pluralistic distribution of political power.

A contrasting view of class conflicts was advocated by Karl Mannheim, who saw the cleavages as ideologically produced, as divergences in modes of thought rather than as rational perception of economic interests. Since Mannheim hoped that such conflicts could be resolved, his doctrine should not be considered fully deterministic, but it did stimulate an effort to interpret the relations between ideas and actions that came to be known as the "sociology of knowledge."

4.11 Mathematical modelism

A variety of efforts has been made to describe and investigate behaviour mathematically, through measurement and counting and the use of mathematical models. This approach in part characterized the early "sociometry" of J.L. Moreno (although its meaning has greatly drifted and broadened in recent years), the "field theory" of Kurt Lewin, and the investigations by George K. Zipf, John Q. Stewart, and others into the relations of rank and size of political units, the frequency of word use in language, and other simple arithmetic relations.

Some of the concepts of game theory, first introduced into economics by its inventors, John von Neumann and Oskar Morgenstern, have also penetrated into sociology. Also the rapidly expanding use of computers has in recent times encouraged the development of various kinds of simulation of behaviour. Some investigations of complex interaction patterns have been carried out by devising games with rules to fit the problem and persons to execute the roles.

When specified rules become highly detailed and complex, the outcome may be sought through the use of a computer; thus the game is converted into a simulation. Sociologists have participated, along with other social scientists, in the creation of such simulations of various political and military processes. Extension of these techniques into a variety of interaction processes is to be expected.

4.12 Sociology of slavery

The slave generally was an outsider. He ordinarily was of a different race, ethnicity, nationality, and religion from his owner. The general rule, as enunciated by the specialist on classical slavery Moses I. Finley, was that "no society could withstand the tension inherent in enslaving its own members." In most cases, the slave was an outsider because he was enslaved against his will in one society and then taken by force to another.

As with nearly all rules, there were exceptions, however. Korea, for reasons that are not understood, was one. India was another exception, because of ritual requirements that the social origins of intimate associates be known; there slaves were ritually distanced from their owners. Muscovite Russia, which had outsider slaves as well, was yet another exception, perhaps because the boundaries between insiders and outsiders were blurred.

A number of scholars have pointed out that, although the status of the slaves was uniformly lower than that of comparable free people in every society, the material and sometimes other conditions of slaves were frequently better than those of free people; thus it is not surprising that free people occasionally volunteered to be slaves.

What is somewhat more surprising is that so few societies found that form of social welfare to be acceptable; most took measures to prohibit or inhibit it. Solon in 594 BC, for example, forbade enslavement for debt in Athens, and the Lex Poetelia Papiria did the same for Rome, *c.* 326 BC. Muscovy in 1597 prevented self-sale into slavery from becoming hereditary by mandating manumission of such slaves on their owners' deaths.

Regardless of the slave's origin, he was nearly always a marginal person in the society in which he was enslaved. In Africa slaves were despised, and their low status, which was passed on to freedmen, persists to the present time. In most societies most slaves were at the very bottom of society.

5. FUNCTIONALISM AND STRUCTURALISM

5.1 Modern major directions of interest

The early schools of thought--each presenting a systematic formulation of sociology that implied possession of exclusive truth and that involved a conviction of the need to destroy rival systems--in time gave way to distinguishable directions of interest and emphasis that did not have to be considered inharmonious. These new directions have no dominant leaders and no clearly defined borderlines.

Following the main contributions in the earlier theoretical formulations of Charles H. Cooley, such later authors as Pitirim A. Sorokin, Talcott Parsons, Robert Merton, Everett C. Hughes, and others have elaborated on the nature of organizations and their relation to the behaviour of persons and have attempted to build workable conceptualizations of very large social systems, nations, and societies.

Sorokin designated his viewpoint as "integralist" and wrote at length about the civilization-cultures that in their balance of values and conditions could be viewed as entities that had distinguishable life cycles, with "ideational," "idealistic," and "sensate" stages marking their growth and decline, thus following a philosophy-of-history tradition shared by Edward Gibbon, Oswald Spengler, and Arnold Toynbee.

Talcott Parsons has given attention to social systems in a more analytical way, inquiring into the conditions that each system must meet in order to survive (the "functional prerequisites"), the character of the standardized and stable interpersonal arrangements (structures) needed to make each system work, the relations to environmental conditions, problems of boundaries, the recruitment and control of members, and the like. Along with Robert Merton and others, he also worked on the classifications of such structures and on distinctions of function.

The subject matter and methods involved in such structural-functional analysis have indeed become so broad that some authors (such as Marion Levy) have held that it becomes synonymous with scientific analysis in general or at least with scientific study of the nature of organization.

On a smaller scale, Kurt Lewin and his co-workers pursued somewhat parallel questions, investigating the nature of small groups, families, professional and military units, looking for arrangements and relationships of the parts of each person's "psychological life space" and of the interrelations of these to a "social space" or society's total range of action. The choice of such relatively small units for research made fruitful experimentation possible, and from Lewin's leadership grew the influential research movement that became known as group dynamics. Some writers have also applied the descriptive term *micro-functionalist* to this tradition.

5.2 Sociometry

Sociometry is used for the measurement techniques used in social psychology, in sociology, and sometimes in social anthropology and psychiatry, based on the assessment of social choice and interpersonal attractiveness. The term is closely associated with the work of the Austrian-born psychiatrist J.L. Moreno, who developed the method as a research and therapeutic technique. Sociometry has come to have several meanings; it is most commonly confined to the quantitative treatment of preferential interpersonal relations, but it is also used to mean the quantitative treatment of all kinds of interpersonal relations. The emphasis may be psychological or sociological.

A sociometric measure assesses the attractions (and sometimes the repulsions) within a given group, usually by having each member of the group specify other persons in the group with whom he would (or would not) like to participate in a given activity. Many variations on this technique exist for studying different aspects of social preference.

Much work has focused on the concept of sociometric status. This includes studies of leadership; of social adjustment, ranging from the social isolate, or unchosen individual, to the sociometric star, or highly chosen; of the relationship between sociometric status and other personality variables, demographic variables, and intelligence; and of minority-group prejudice.

5.3 Europe and social sciences

In the social sciences, fresh starts were made on new premises. Anthropology dropped its concern with physique and race and turned to "culture" as the proper unit of scientific study.

Similarly in sociology, Durkheim, seconded by Tönnies, Weber, Tarde, and Le Bon, concentrated on "the social fact" as an independent and measurable reality equivalent to a physical datum. Psychology, also long under the exclusive sway of physics and physiology, now established at the hands of William James that the irreducible element of its subject matter was the "stream of consciousness"--not a compound of atomized "ideas" or "impressions" or "mind-stuff" but a live force in which image and feeling, subconscious drive and purposive interest, were not separable except abstractly.

A last domain of research was mythology, to the significance of which James George Frazer's *The Golden Bough* gave massive witness, thereby exerting proportional influence on literature and criticism.

5.4 Theoretical modes

There are a few social scientists who maintain that interest in theory is a casualty of the 20th-century fascination with method and fact. Though there is a great deal less of that grand or comprehensive theory that was a hallmark of 19th-century social philosophy and social science, there are still those persons occasionally to be found today who are engrossed in search for master principles, for general and unified theory that will assimilate all the lesser and more specialized types of theory. But their efforts and results are not regarded as successful by the vast majority of social scientists.

Theory, at its best, today tends to be specific theory--related to one or other of the major divisions of research within each of the social sciences. The theory of the firm in economics, of deviance in sociology, of communication in political science, of attitude formation in social psychology, of divergent development in cultural anthropology are all examples of theory in every proper sense of the word. But each is, clearly, specific. If there is a single social science in which a more or less unified theory exists, with reference to the whole of the discipline, it is economics. Even here, however, unified, general theory does not have the sovereign sweep it had in the classical tradition of Ricardo and his followers before the true complexities of economic behaviour had become revealed.

5.5 Social role

Role in sociology is the behaviour expected of an individual who occupies a given social position or status. A role is a comprehensive pattern of behaviour that is socially recognized, providing a means of identifying and placing an individual in a society. It also serves as a strategy for coping with recurrent situations and dealing with the roles of others (*e.g.*, parent-child roles).

The term, borrowed from theatrical usage, emphasizes the distinction between the actor and the part. A role remains relatively stable even though different people occupy the position: any individual assigned the role of physician, like any actor in the role of Hamlet, is expected to behave in a particular way. An individual may have a unique style, but this is exhibited within the boundaries of the expected behaviour.

Role expectations include both actions and qualities: a teacher may be expected not only to deliver lectures, assign homework, and prepare examinations but also to be dedicated, concerned, honest, and responsible. Individuals usually occupy several positions, which may or may not be compatible with one another: one person may be husband, father, artist, and patient, with each role entailing certain obligations, duties, privileges, and rights vis-à-vis other persons.

5.6 Sociolinguistics

Just as it is difficult to draw the boundary between linguistics and psycholinguistics and between psychology and psycholinguistics, so it is difficult to distinguish sharply between linguistics and sociolinguistics and between sociolinguistics and sociology. There is the further difficulty that, because the boundary between sociology and anthropology is also unclear, sociolinguistics merges with anthropological linguistics (see below).

It is frequently suggested that there is a conflict between the sociolinguistic and the psycholinguistic approach to the study of language, and it is certainly the case that two distinct points of view are discernible in the literature at the present time. Chomsky has described linguistics as a branch of cognitive psychology, and neither he nor most of his followers have yet shown much interest in the relationship between language and its social and cultural matrix.

On the other hand, many modern schools of linguistics that have been very much concerned with the role of language in society would tend to relate linguistics more closely to sociology and anthropology than to any other discipline. It would seem that the opposition between the psycholinguistic and the sociolinguistic viewpoint must ultimately be transcended. The acquisition of language, a topic of central concern to psycholinguists, is in part dependent upon and in part itself determines the process of socialization; and the ability to use one's native language correctly in the numerous socially prescribed situations of daily life is as characteristic a feature of linguistic competence, in the broad sense of this term, as is the ability to produce grammatical utterances.

Some of the most recent work in sociolinguistics and psycholinguistics has sought to widen the notion of linguistic competence in this way. So far, however, sociolinguistics and psycholinguistics tend to be regarded as relatively independent areas of research.

5.7 Russell's Assessment

Bertrand Russell had one of the most widely varied and persistently influential intellects of the 20th century. During most of his active life, a span of three generations, Russell had at any time more than 40 books in print ranging over philosophy, mathematics, science, ethics, sociology, education, history, religion, politics, and polemic.

The extent of his influence resulted partly from his amazing efficiency in applying his intellect (he normally wrote at the rate of 3,000 largely unaltered words a day) and partly from the deep humanitarian feeling that was the mainspring of his actions. This feeling expressed itself consistently at the frontier of social change through what he himself would have called a liberal anarchistic, left-wing, and sceptical atheist temperament.

5.8 Freudian influences

In the general area of personality, mind, and character, the writings of Sigmund Freud have had influence on 20th-century culture and thought scarcely less than Marx's. His basic theories of the role of the unconscious mind, of the lasting effects of infantile sexuality, and of the Oedipus complex have gone beyond the discipline of psychoanalysis and even the larger area of psychiatry to areas of several of the social sciences.

Anthropologists have applied Freudian concepts to their studies of primitive cultures, seeking to assess comparatively the universality of states of the unconscious that Freud and his followers held to lie in the whole human race. Some political scientists have used Freudian ideas to illuminate the nature of authority generally and political power specifically, seeing in totalitarianism, for example, the thrust of a craving for the security that total power can give. Sociology and social psychology have been influenced by Freudian ideas in their studies of social interaction and motivation.

From Freud came the fruitful perspective that sees social behaviour and attitudes as generated not merely by the external situation but also by internal emotional needs springing from childhood--needs for recognition, authority, and self-expression.

Whatever may be the place directly occupied by Freud's ideas in the social sciences today, his influence upon 20th-century thought and culture generally, not excluding the social sciences, has been hardly less than Marx's.

5.9 Old age

Old age, also called senescence. This, in human beings is the final stage of the normal life span. Definitions of old age are not consistent with reference to biology, demography (conditions of mortality and morbidity), employment and retirement, and sociology. For statistical and public administrative purposes, however, old age is frequently defined as 60 or 65 years of age or older.

Old age has a dual definition. It is the last stage in the life processes of an individual, and it is an age group or generation comprising a segment of the oldest members of a population. The social aspects of old age are influenced by the relationship of the physiological effects of aging and the collective experiences and shared values of that generation to the particular organization of the society in which it exists.

There is no universally accepted age that is considered old among or within societies. Often discrepancies exist as to what age a society may consider old and what members in that society of that age and older may consider old. Moreover, biologists are not in agreement about the existence of an inherent biological cause for aging. However, presently in most Western countries, 60 or 65 is the age of eligibility for retirement and old-age social programs, although many countries and societies regard old age as occurring anywhere from the mid-40s to the 70s.

5.10 Social change

In sociology, this is the alteration of mechanisms within the social structure, characterized by changes in cultural symbols, rules of behaviour, or value systems.

Throughout its historical development, sociology has borrowed models of social change from other fields. In the late 19th century, when evolution became the predominant model for understanding biological change, ideas of social change took on an evolutionary cast, and, though other models have refined modern notions of social change, evolution remains often an underlying principle.

Other sociological models created analogies between social change and the West's technological progress. In the mid-20th century, anthropologists borrowed from the theory of structuralism to elaborate an approach to social change called structural functionalism. This theory postulated the existence of certain basic institutions (including kinship relations and division of labour) that determine social behaviour. Change in one institution affects other institutions because they function interdependently.

Marxist economic theory concluded that social change is the result of various social classes within a culture vying for power. This conflict theory and the structural-functional theory represent two sides of the same coin. Although both agree that social change and structure are mutually interdependent, the conflict model stresses the process of change while the structural-functional model focuses on the elements of stability.

Social change can evolve from a number of different sources, including changes in the ecosystem (which can cause the loss of natural resources or widespread disease); technological change (epitomized by the Industrial Revolution, which created a new social group, the urban proletariat); population growth and other demographic variables; and ideological, economic, and political movements.

5.11 Population

In human biology this is the whole number of inhabitants occupying an area (such as a country or the world) and continually being modified by increases (births and immigrations) and losses (deaths and emigrations). As with any biological population, the size of a human population is limited by the supply of food, the effect of diseases, and other environmental factors. Human populations are further affected by social customs governing reproduction and by the technological developments, especially in medicine and public health that have reduced mortality and extended the life span.

Few aspects of human societies are as fundamental as the size, composition, and rate of change of their populations. Such factors affect economic prosperity, health, education, family structure, crime patterns, language, and culture--indeed, virtually every aspect of human society is touched upon by population trends.

The study of human populations is called demography--a discipline with intellectual origins stretching back to the 18th century, when it was first recognized that human mortality could be examined as a phenomenon with statistical regularities. Demography casts a multidisciplinary net, drawing insights from economics, sociology, statistics, medicine, biology, anthropology, and history.

Its chronological sweep is lengthy: limited demographic evidence for many centuries into the past and reliable data for several hundred years are available for many regions. The present understanding of demography makes it possible to project (with caution) population changes several decades into the future.

6. DATA COLLECTION

6.1 Research categories

Within the main categories of research methods there are many special problems for which techniques have been devised. Data collection, for example, is effected in many different ways, from unstructured observation, essentially methodless, to sophisticated measurement through special instruments. Some of the basic problems of data collection concern such matters as the most efficient use of terminology, the definitions of units to be measured, and the classifications to be used.

In general it is necessary to consider the nature of a specific problem in order to choose the most appropriate unit. For example, in a study of the relation of the size of a city to the cost of operating its local government, the proper unit might well be the population residing within its political boundaries. If the research question, however, is the relation of city size to any of a number of forms of social disorganization, it may be more fruitful to recognize that sociologically the significant unit would include much or all of the settled areas outside the city limits.

6.2 Differentiations

In the fields of social differentiation and occupational mobility the matter of definition of specific occupations is critical. If persons are asked in a questionnaire to state their occupation, the usual response is to give only one occupation, and this one is sometimes vaguely defined and made obscure by the tendency to give a euphemistic answer.

Persons change occupations; some have more than one; some might claim an occupation that they merely aspire to. The art of obtaining useful answers to such important questions involves carefully designed questions adapted to the specific purposes of the study. General classifications, intended for a variety of studies, have limited utility.

In the process of gathering research data for sociology there are occasional obstacles to direct observation. In such cases indirect indicators may provide crude but useful substitutes. For example, alcoholic consumption in a small village in which the beverage is supposed to be prohibited may be estimated by a count of empty bottles in trash receptacles, or perhaps in the town dump. Library book circulation has been used to estimate the use of television in a community in which withdrawals of books of fiction declined, while non-fiction withdrawals remained as before.

6.3 Questionnaires

Questionnaires are convenient for obtaining information from large numbers of respondents but involve many methodological problems.

Wording of questions must of course be intelligible to uneducated and uninterested persons, must have standard meanings to persons of varying backgrounds, must avoid topics that arouse resistance and refusal to complete the questionnaire, and must avoid being too complex or difficult so that returns are insufficient or constitute a biased sample.

Since it is known that slight alterations in the wording of questionnaire items may produce considerable variations in the pattern of responses, the precise wording becomes a matter of some art as well as science. A similar effect occurs in the order of items, since some may suggest or influence responses on later ones.

Similar issues are involved in data gathering through interviewing. It is necessary to control such variables as the appearance, manner, and approach of the interviewer, the specific manner in which questions are asked, ways of avoiding interviewer influence on the responses, and the tendency of some respondents to refuse to answer questions or to discontinue the interview.

To meet the problems of resistance on sensitive subjects and inarticulateness about some feelings, various indirect or projective devices may be employed so that a respondent in answering one question provides information he may not realize he is giving about other questions.

Questionnaires and interviews may be so arranged that the patterns of responses form a scale, converting qualitative variations into measures available for statistical treatment. An early scaling method, devised in the late 1920s by a psychologist, L.L. Thurstone, is still widely used in sociology.

It is formed in the following way: a list of questionnaire items is presented to a number of judges who independently re-list the items in the order in which they consider them important or of interest. From their decisions are selected items on which there is satisfactory agreement of scale value.

Scaling may also be provided by statements to which a respondent is asked whether he "strongly approves," "approves," is "undecided," "disapproves," or "strongly disapproves." Or the quantitative differences may be introduced through a logical sequence of preference answers--for example, whether the respondent would admit a particular category of person (a) to close kinship by marriage, (b) to his club as a personal chum, (c) to employment in his occupation, (d) to citizenship in his country. Here it is assumed that the later answers imply more desired social distance.

6.4 Class of methods

A method or class of methods called sociometry has been under development since its introduction in the middle 1930s by J.L. Moreno. The essence of the method is the collection and tabulation of information about various types of interaction among members of groups of small or moderate size. The interaction may be either actual behaviour or merely anticipated or desired behaviour, and it may consist of preferences for various kinds of association with other persons, such as having them as friends, sitting with them, working with them, and the like.

The information may be collected by observation of real behaviour or by interviews or questionnaires with specific items regarding personal choices. After the information is gathered, it is sometimes put in the form of a sociogram, consisting of names of persons enclosed in circles or squares distributed over an area and connected with lines and arrows that indicate both detail of choices and general patterns of relationships.

A person receiving many choices is readily seen as the target end of many lines and is sometimes referred to as a "star." A person completely unchosen has no lines pointing toward his name and is called an isolate. Further investigation of persons typed in this fashion may be made by statistical methods, case studies, or otherwise. Overall, it can be said that various improvements and elaborations of the basic sociometric approach have been made, and the method is now less distinctively separate from other social psychology research than it was originally.

6.5 Cultural and social geography

Five major themes characterize cultural geography: culture, culture area, cultural landscape, cultural history, and cultural ecology.

The cultural geographer studies the distribution in space and time of cultures and the elements of culture, such as artefacts and tools, techniques, attitudes, customs, languages, and religious beliefs; cultural complexes in their spatial organization; the cultural landscape--*i.e.*, the association of human, biologic, and physical features on the surface of the Earth (especially as perceived visually), ranging from the natural landscape unaffected by humankind to the landscape as thoroughly transformed by human action; the evolution and succession of cultures and cultural elements, including the history of cultural origins and their areal diffusion; and the complex interrelationships and areal associations of culture and nature.

The American geographer Carl O. Sauer was particularly creative in working the concepts and teaching of anthropology, archaeology, and sociology into geography.

Whereas the focus of cultural geography is more on traditional societies (though it is not restricted to them), social geography is more oriented toward urban problems in countries with advanced economies. Social geographers have been concerned particularly with the spatial aspects of disadvantaged groups (such as minorities, women, the aged, and the poor), of such social pathologies as crime and mental illness, and of inequality, social welfare, and housing.

6.6 Social structure

Social structure in sociology is the distinctive arrangement of institutions whereby human beings in a society interact and are able to live together. Social structure is often treated together with the concept of social change, which deals with the forces that change society and the social structure itself.

Social structure and social change are general concepts used by social scientists, particularly in the fields of sociology and social and cultural anthropology. They are often conceived of as polarized twin concepts, social structure referring to permanence, social change to the opposite. The relationship between the two concepts is, however, more complicated. "Structure," for instance, does not necessarily indicate lack of change.

Those features of a society, or any other social group, that are regarded as parts of its structure are always generated by dynamic processes. For example, the kinship structure of a given society (the typical composition of household units and the rules governing marriage and line of descent) is maintained by continuous changes in families, as marriages are concluded; children are born, grow up, and become adults; and people die. Second, although many social processes show a cyclical pattern--the formation, dissolution, and reformation of families being one example--social life never repeats itself completely.

The kinship relations in one generation are never an exact replica of those in the previous one. The same processes that serve to maintain the social structure may also lead to social change and modification of the structure over a long period.

The concepts of social structure and social change pertain not only to basic characteristics of human social life but also to certain ideals and preferences. The structure, or order, of the society, generally regarded as harmonious and conducive to the general well-being, has also been seen as conflict-ridden and repressive.

Similarly, social change has been conceived of both as progress and as decay, as emancipation on the one hand and as deviance from good tradition on the other. Such widely varying evaluations have influenced different theories concerning the nature of social structure and social change, and they continue to be reflected, to some extent, in present-day social thought.

6.7 Interest groups

Studies of interest groups, elites, and political parties also have their own independent origins, although they, too, have been brought within the framework of systems analysis. Interest groups and political parties, for example, have been described as agencies for the articulation and aggregation of interests, which in turn provide inputs (demands) for the political system to convert into outputs (decisions and actions). But interest-group analysis antedates the advent of behaviouralism.

The modern concern for the subject starts perhaps with studies of prohibition and other pressure groups during the 1920s. More generalized and theoretical treatments of interest groups and political parties resulted in part from a revived interest in the work of Bentley in the 1930s and 1950s.

The study of elites was begun at least as early as 1936 (Lasswell's "influentials"), and it came to the forefront in the 1950s in community studies made by political scientists in Atlanta, Chicago, New York, New Haven, and elsewhere. Such studies had long been familiar in sociology, but they acquired special significance in political science, because democratic values seemed threatened by the possible existence of elites. Despite declarations of their concern to establish a value-free science, American political scientists have thus tended to cleave to the traditional democratic ethic, in which elites are presumed to have no place.

6.8 Philosophy of mind

In distinguishing the field of philosophy of mind from other sorts of investigation, one immediately obvious feature is its subject matter, the nature of mind and its various manifestations. This serves to distinguish it from empirical sciences such as astronomy and physics, which study matter in motion; from formal disciplines such as geometry and algebra, which study mathematical relationships; and from other fields of philosophy such as the philosophy of art and the philosophy of law.

But subject matter alone does not serve to distinguish the philosophy of mind, since the mind is the subject of investigation of other disciplines as well--especially of psychology and of certain phases of biology, physiology, sociology, and anthropology. In comparison with these fields, it is by its method that the philosophy of mind is to be distinguished; for it proceeds not by the methods of empirical investigation--detailed sense observation, the formulation of predictions, the construction of experiments, inductive confirmation, the inventing and testing of contingent generalizations, theories, and laws--but by the method of philosophical reflection.

That method consists of the examination of meanings, the analysis and clarification of concepts, the search for necessary truths, the use of deductive inference, reductio ad absurdum, and arguments with infinitely repeating terms and other forms of a priori reasoning, and the attempt to arrive at and evaluate the fundamental principles that underlie and justify the basic forms of human thought and endeavour.

Although the philosophy of mind is a distinct field of investigation, it has many important relations with other fields. First, its methods, being those of philosophy in general, are to be tested by the fruits that they have yielded in other areas: if a method has been successful in other areas, it is reasonable to try it here; if unsuccessful in other areas, it is suspect here. Second, the conclusions achieved in such fields as epistemology, metaphysics, logic, ethics, and the philosophy of religion are quite relevant to the philosophy of mind; and its conclusions, in turn, have important implications for those fields.

Moreover, this reciprocity applies as well to its relations to such empirical disciplines as neurology, psychology, sociology, and history. Thus, the philosopher of mind must keep informed of developments in all related fields of investigation.

6.9 Behavioural persuasion

In American political science since the end of World War II, the behavioural persuasion has been the dominant one. A former president of the American Political Science Association has attributed the rapid development of the behavioural approach to six causes: the inspiration of the Chicago school; the immigration to the United States in the 1930s of large numbers of European scholars (particularly Germans) with backgrounds in European sociology, who stressed the relevance of sociology to politics; the movement of many political scientists into administrative and political positions during World War II; the influence of foundation support in the encouragement of research in political behaviour; the increasing development of the survey method in certain political studies, such as voter behaviour; and the missionary work of the Social Science Research Council under leadership sympathetic to behaviouralism.

Although the term behaviouralism has been freely used in political-science writings, there is in fact confusion as to whether it is a field of study, a method, or an approach. One American political scientist, Heinz Eulau, in *The Behavioural Persuasion in Politics* (1963), has said that the behavioural persuasion "is concerned with what man does politically and the meanings he attaches to his behavior," and he has suggested that researchers cannot afford to get tangled up in problems of definition. Another American, Robert Dahl, has said that it is a mood or even "the scientific outlook."

The term behavioural, then, may be merely a term having distinctiveness, weight, and value for a certain time only, since it seems primarily to signify that phase in the quarter century after World War II during which there was a significant revival of interest in empirical studies in politics, a movement strong enough to establish at least a partnership with the traditional approaches, although some of its advocates have gone so far as to say that their science has made traditional approaches outdated.

6.10 Criminal law

Criminal law has been strongly influenced in the past century or two by the social sciences, especially criminology, sociology, and psychology. The empirical methods of the social sciences have been introduced into legal research and have done much to improve legislation and the courts' approach to sentencing, as well as the planning methods of law-enforcement agencies.

The fact that the crime rates in many countries have risen faster than the population has brought into question the relevance of the law itself and whether or not laws against crime actually have an influence on an individual's behaviour. Various large-scale inquiries have been made into the relation between law and civil order: in the United States, the President's Commission on Law Enforcement and Administration of Justice; in Europe, several research studies sponsored by the Council of Europe; in Germany, the hearings of the Criminal Reform Commission of the Bundestag.

One conclusion emerging from these inquiries is that criminal legislation ought to be restricted to acts that pose a serious threat to public order and that can be effectively dealt with by the police, the courts, and various correctional institutions. The effort to punish all behaviour that is considered immoral or deviant, such as drunkenness, gambling, disorderly conduct, vagrancy, and petty sex offences, simply multiplies the number of crimes without changing the norms of behaviour.

7. ROLE OF PERSONAL OR SOCIAL FACTORS

7.1 Metaphysical outlook

Some writers on the philosophy of philosophy, such as Dilthey, have suggested that the persistence of a plurality of metaphysical systems is to be explained in terms of personal or social factors. Certain kinds of metaphysical outlook appeal to certain types of human being, or gain currency in social circumstances of this kind or that; to understand why they are accepted, recourse must be had to psychology or sociology or both. In the above account, stress has been laid on the historical background against which a number of famous metaphysical theories got their classical formulations; it is idle to deny that each was originally designed to solve a problem deemed to be urgent at the time.

Nevertheless, the problem was, of course, an intellectual problem, and the solution offered claimed to be true, not simply comforting. No doubt wishful thinking is as rife in the field of metaphysics as anywhere; it is all too easy here to confuse what men ought to believe with what they want to believe. Philosophies reveal something about their authors and even about their historical age, as works of literature do; they constitute historical evidence as books on mathematics, perhaps, do not.

Yet all this can be admitted without agreeing that metaphysics is merely of psychological or historical importance. Science does not cease to be true because it is shown to be useful. Nor is it true that metaphysical theories always in fact give comfort; there are cases in which men find themselves returning over and over again to possibilities that they would very much like to believe were not realized.

A philosopher can commit himself to a view of the world that is not at all to his taste, simply because it seems to him on due consideration that this is how things are. That philosophers are godlike beings able to rise entirely above the limitations of their age seems unlikely. It is equally unlikely, however, that their opinions are determined throughout by non-rational factors, and thus that their thinking can lay no claim to truth.

7.2 Basic aims and methods

The growth of various disciplines in the 19th century, notably psychology and sociology, stimulated a more analytic approach to religions, while at the same time theology became more sophisticated and, in a sense, scientific as it began to be affected by and thus to make use of historical and other methods. The interrelations of the various disciplines in relation to religion as an area of study can be described as follows.

Religions, being complex, have different aspects or dimensions. Thus, the major world religions typically possess doctrines, myths, ethical and social teachings, rituals, social institutions, and inner experiences and sentiments. These dimensions lie behind the creation of buildings, art, music, and other such extensions of basic beliefs and attitudes. But not all religions are like Christianity and Buddhism, for example, in possessing institutions such as the church and the *sangha* (Buddhist monastic order), which exist across national and cultural boundaries. In opposition to such institutionalized religions, tribal religion, for example, is not usually separately institutionalized but in effect is the religious side of communal life and is not treated as distinct from other things that go on in the community.

The various dimensions of religion noted above represent a cross section of a tradition; but to see the latter in a well-balanced perspective it is necessary to view it as historical--as a religion having a past and the capacity for development in the future ("dead" religions, obviously enough, being the exception).

Thus, there are various disciplines that may examine a religion cross-sectionally to find its basic patterns or structures. Psychology views religious experience and feelings and to some extent the myths and symbols that express experience; sociology and social anthropology view the institutions of religious tradition and their relationship to its beliefs and values; and literary and other studies seek to elicit the meanings of myths and other items.

These structural enquiries sometimes benefit from being comparative--as when recurrent motifs in the doctrines of different religions are noticed. On the other hand, the aforementioned disciplines need to be supplemented by history, archaeology, philology, and other such disciplines, which have their own various methods of elucidating the past. Philosophy generally has attempted wide-ranging accounts of the nature of religion and of religious concepts, but it is not always easy to disentangle these enquiries from issues raised by normative theology.

7.3 Social norm

In sociology, norm, social norm, rule or standard of behaviour is shared by members of a social group. Norms may be internalized--*i.e.,* incorporated within the individual so that there is conformity without external rewards or punishments, or they may be enforced by positive or negative sanctions from without. The social unit sharing particular norms may be small (*e.g.,* a clique of friends) or may include all adult members of a society. Norms are more specific than values or ideals: honesty is a general value, but the rules defining what honest behaviour in a particular situation is are norms.

There are two schools of thought regarding why people conform to norms. The functionalist school of sociology maintains that norms reflect a consensus, a common value system developed through socialization, the process by which an individual learns the culture of his group. Norms contribute to the functioning of the social system and are said to develop to meet certain assumed "needs" of the system. The conflict school holds that norms are a mechanism for dealing with recurring social problems.

The Marxian variety of conflict theory states that norms reflect the power of one section of a society over the other sections and that coercion and sanctions maintain these rules. Norms are thought to originate as a means by which one class or caste dominates or exploits others. Neither school adequately explains differences between and within societies.

Norm is also used to mean a statistically determined standard or the average behaviour, attitude, or opinion of a social group. In this sense it means actual, rather than expected, behaviour.

7.4 Canon law and its sources

Because of the discontinuity that has developed between church and state in modern times and the more exclusively spiritual and pastoral function of church organization, scholars in canon law are searching for a recovery of vital contact among canon law and theology, biblical exegesis (critical interpretive principles of the Bible), and church history in their contemporary forms.

Canon-law scholars are also seeking a link with the empirical social sciences (e.g., sociology, anthropology, and other such disciplines), which is required for insight into and control of the application of canon law. The study of the history of canon law calls not only for juridical and historical training but also for insight into contemporary theological concepts and social relationships.

Many sources, such as the documents of councils and popes, are often uncritical and found only in badly organized publications, and much of the material exists only in manuscripts and archives; frequently the legal sources contain dead law (i.e., law no longer held valid) and say nothing about living law.

What does and does not come under canon law, what is or is not a source of canon law, which law is universal and which local, and other such questions must be judged differently for different periods.

The function of canon law in liturgy, preaching, and social activities involves the development and maintenance of those institutions that are considered to be most serviceable for the personal life and faith of members of the church and for their vocation in the world. This function is thus concerned with a continual adaptation of canon law to the circumstances of the time as well as to personal needs.

7.5 Slang sources

Most subcultures tend to draw words and phrases from the contiguous language (rather than creating many new words) and to give these established terms new and special meanings; some borrowings from foreign languages, including the American Indian tongues are traditional.

The more learned occupations or professions like medicine, law, psychology, sociology, engineering, and electronics tend to create true neologisms, often based on Greek or Latin roots, but these are not major sources for slang, though nurses and medical students adapt some medical terminology to their slang, and air force personnel and some other branches of the armed services borrow freely from engineering and electronics.

7.6 Linguistic processes

The processes by which words become slang are the same as those by which other words in the language change their form or meaning or both. Some of these are the employment of metaphor, simile, folk etymology, distortion of sounds in words, generalization, specialization, clipping, the use of acronyms, elevation and degeneration, metonymy, synecdoche, hyperbole, borrowings from foreign languages, and the play of euphemism against taboo.

The English word trip is an example of a term that has undergone both specialization and generalization. It first became specialized to mean a psychedelic experience resulting from the drug LSD. Subsequently, it generalized again to mean any experience on any drug, and beyond that to any type of "kicks" from anything. Clipping is exemplified by the use of "grass" from "laughing grass," a term for marijuana. "Funky," once a very low term for body odour, has undergone elevation among jazz buffs to signify "the best"; "fanny," on the other hand, once simply a girl's name, is currently a degenerated term that refers to the buttocks (in England, it has further degenerated into a taboo word for the female genitalia). There is also some actual coinage of slang terms.

7.7 Functionalism

In social sciences, this is the theory based on the premise that all aspects of a society--institutions, roles, norms, etc.--serve a purpose and that all are indispensable for the long-term survival of the society. The approach gained prominence in the works of 19th-century sociologists, particularly those who viewed societies as organisms. The French sociologist Émile

Durkheim argued that it was necessary to understand the "needs" of the social organism to which social phenomena correspond.

Other writers have used the concept of function to mean the interrelationships of parts within a system, the adaptive aspect of a phenomenon, or its observable consequences. In sociology, functionalism met the need for a method of analysis; in anthropology it provided an alternative to evolutionary theory and trait-diffusion analysis.

A social system is assumed to have a functional unity in which all parts of the system work together with some degree of internal consistency. Functionalism also postulates that all cultural or social phenomena have a positive function and that all are indispensable. Distinctions have been made between manifest functions, those consequences intended and recognized by participants in the system, and latent functions, which are neither intended nor recognized.

The British anthropologist A.R. Radcliffe-Brown explored the theoretical implications of functionalism as a relationship between a social institution and the "necessary conditions of existence" of a social system. He saw the function of a unit as the contribution it makes to the maintenance of a social structure--*i.e.*, the set of relationships among social units.

In an attempt to develop a more dynamic analysis of social systems, the American sociologist Talcott Parsons introduced a structural-functional approach that employs the concept of function as a link between relatively stable structural categories. Any process or set of conditions that does not contribute to the maintenance or development of the system is said to be dysfunctional. In particular, there is a focus on the conditions of stability, integration, and effectiveness of the system.

7.8 Cross-cultural perspective

A further problem about the multidisciplinary study of religion is that little has been done to explore the problem of the people to whom religions are interpreted--the clientele for the subject. Hitherto, the main assumption has been that the study is for Westerners, though a number of distinguished Asian and African scholars are working in the field.

Until recently, owing to the unequal cultural and political relationship between Western and non-Western religions, however, some of the most vital contributions have been primarily attempts to articulate (for the new apologetic situation) the old traditions. This has been a main concern of scholars of Asian religions such as Sarvepalli Radhakrishnan, T.R.V. Murti, and K.N. Jayatilleke. The prospect is, however, that an intellectual community will be the clientele of the subject. To this extent the study of religions will most likely involve, as it does already to some extent, a complex dialogue between religions.

Another problem is the need to elucidate the basis of a dynamic typology of religion in which phenomenology and history are properly brought together. The tendency toward a rift between the historians and phenomenologists is unnecessary and causes harm to the pursuit of the subject.

Meanwhile, some emergent tendencies within the various disciplines can be perceived. There is an increased concern in anthropological theory for the content of religious symbolism, such as in the work of the English anthropologist Mary Douglas; and the sociology of religion is, in a sense, returning to the method of Max Weber in stressing the comparison of cultures. The important development of Oriental and African studies since World War II has made this task easier--American sociologists have, for example, examined in some detail Japanese culture and religion.

The interest in symbolism and mythology coincides with developments in the philosophy of religion, which, under the influence of Wittgenstein (in his later, more open phase), is concerned with explicating different functions of language. One area of the study of religion that is seriously underdeveloped at the present time--other than in respect to the psychoanalytic approaches--is the psychology of religion, although current interest in mysticism and other forms of religious experience has stimulated the collection and interpretation of data. One of the difficult problems to be solved is the extent to which cultural conditioning exerts an influence on the actual content of such experience.

In many ways the present position promises well for an expanding multidisciplinary approach to problems in the study of religion. Historians of religion are recognizing some of the contributions to be made by modern sociology, and sociologists--partly because of the development of the sociology of knowledge--have become more aware of the need for accounting for the particular systems of meaning in religion. An area that may very well exhibit the new synthesis is the study of new religious movements.

After a period of relative unconcern, Christian theology is increasingly aware of the challenge of other religious beliefs, so that there are greater impulses toward blending Christian and other studies--often kept rather artificially apart, though biblical studies, especially Old Testament studies, have usually been quite closely related to the history of the relevant religions of the ancient Middle East.

Meanwhile, in a number of Western countries (chiefly in Europe, but also to some extent in the United States), the study of religion on a pluralistic and multidisciplinary basis is being increasingly viewed as an important element in the education of secondary school students. This, together with the popularity of the subject in universities, may ensure that the study of religion will increase in significance.

7.9 Physical and cultural anthropology

Here, anthropology is explained as a distinction of two large disciplines-- physical anthropology and cultural anthropology--and such related disciplines as prehistory and linguistics now cover the program that originally was set up for a single study of anthropology.

The two fields are largely autonomous, having their own relations with disciplines outside anthropology; and it is unlikely that any researchers today work simultaneously in the fields of physical and cultural anthropology. The generalist has become rare. On the other hand, the fields have not been cut off from one another. Specialists in the two fields still cooperate in specific genetic or demographic problems and other matters.

Prehistoric archaeology and linguistics also have notable links with cultural anthropology. In posing the problem of the evolution of mankind in an inductive way, archaeology contributed to the creation of the first concepts of anthropology, and archaeology is still indispensable in uncovering the past of societies under observation. In many areas, when it is a question of interpreting the use of rudimentary tools or of certain elementary religious phenomena, prehistory and cultural anthropology are mutually helpful. "Primitive" societies that have not yet reached the metal age are still in existence.

Relations between linguistics and cultural anthropology are numerous. On a purely practical level the cultural anthropologist has to serve a linguistic apprenticeship. He cannot do without knowledge of the language of the people he is studying, and often he has had to make the first survey of it. One of his essential tasks, moreover, has been to collect the various forms of oral expression, including myths, folk tales, proverbs, and so forth. On the theoretical level, cultural anthropology has often used concepts developed in the field of linguistics: in studying society as a system of communication, in defining the notion of structure, and in analyzing the way in which man organizes and classifies his whole experience of the world.

Cultural anthropology maintains relations with a great number of other sciences. It has been said of sociology, for instance, that it was almost the twin sister of anthropology. The two are presumably differentiated by their field of study (modern societies versus traditional societies). But the contrast is forced. These two social sciences often meet. Thus, the study of colonial societies borrows as much from sociology as from cultural anthropology. And it has already been remarked how cultural anthropology intervenes more and more frequently in urban and industrial fields classically the domain of sociology.

There have also been fruitful exchanges with other disciplines quite distinct from cultural anthropology. In political science the discussion of the concept of the state and of its origin has been nourished by cultural anthropology. Economists, too, have depended on cultural anthropology to see concepts in a more comparative light and even to challenge the very notion of an "economic man" (suspiciously similar to the 19th-century capitalist revered by the classical economists).

Cultural anthropology has brought to psychology new bases on which to reflect on concepts of personality and the formation of personality. It has permitted psychology to develop a system of cross-cultural psychiatry, or so-called ethno-psychiatry. Conversely, the psychological sciences, particularly psychoanalysis, have offered cultural anthropology new hypotheses for an interpretation of the concept of culture.

The link with history has long been a vital one because cultural anthropology was originally based on an evolutionist point of view and because it has striven to reconstruct the cultural history of societies about which, for lack of written documents, no historical record could be determined. Cultural anthropology has more recently suggested to historians new techniques of research based on the analysis and criticism of oral tradition. And so "ethno-history" is beginning to emerge. Finally, cultural anthropology has close links with human geography. Both of them place great importance on man either as he uses space or acts to transform the natural environment. It is not without significance that some early anthropologists were originally geographers.

8. SOCIAL PSYCHOLOGY AND RELATED DICIPLINES

8.1 Social behaviour

Social psychology is the scientific study of the behaviour of individuals in their social and cultural setting. Although the term may be taken to include the social activity of laboratory animals or those in the wild, the emphasis here is on human social behaviour.

Once a relatively speculative, intuitive enterprise, social psychology has become an active form of empirical investigation, the volume of research literature having risen rapidly after about 1925. Social psychologists now have a substantial volume of observation data covering a range of topics; the evidence remains loosely coordinated, however, and the field is beset by many different theories and conceptual schemes.

Early impetus in research came from the United States, and much work in other countries has followed U.S. tradition, though independent research efforts are being made elsewhere in the world. Social psychology is being actively pursued in the United Kingdom, Canada, Australia, Germany, The Netherlands, France, Belgium, Scandinavia, Japan, and Russia. Most social psychologists are members of university departments of psychology; others are in departments of sociology or work in such applied settings as industry and government.

Much research in social psychology has consisted of laboratory experiments on social behaviour, but this approach has been criticized in recent years as being too stultifying, artificial, and unrealistic. Much of the conceptual background of research in social psychology derives from other fields of psychology. While learning theory and psychoanalysis were once most influential, cognitive and linguistic approaches to research have become more popular; sociological contributions also have been influential.

Social psychologists are employed, or used as consultants, in setting up the social organization of businesses and psychiatric communities; some work to reduce racial conflict, to design mass communications (*e.g.*, advertising), and to advise on child rearing. They have helped in the treatment of mental patients and in the rehabilitation of convicts. Fundamental research in social psychology has been brought to the attention of the public through popular books and in the periodical press.

8.2 Specializations

A major point to make about the social sciences of the 20th century is the vast increase in the number of social scientists involved, in the number of academic and other centres of teaching and research in the social sciences, and in their degree of both comprehensiveness and specialization. The explosion of the sciences generally in the 20th century--an explosion responsible for the fact that a majority of all scientists who have ever lived in human history are now alive--has had, as one of its signal elements, the explosion of the social sciences. Not only has there been development and proliferation but there has also been a spectacular diffusion of the social sciences.

Beginning in a few places in western Europe and the United States in the 19th century, the social sciences, as bodies of ongoing research and centres of teaching, are today to be found almost everywhere in the world. In considerable part this has followed the spread of universities from the West to other parts of the world and, within universities, the very definite shift away from the hegemony once held by humanities alone to the near-hegemony held today by the sciences, physical and social.

Specialization has been as notable a tendency in the social sciences as in the biological and physical sciences. This is reflected not only in varieties of research but also in course offerings in academic departments. Whereas not very many years ago, a couple of dozen advanced courses in a social science reflected the specialization and diversity of the discipline even in major universities with graduate schools, today a hundred such courses are found to be not enough.

Side by side with this strong trend toward specialization, however, is another, countering trend: that of cross-fertilization and interdisciplinary cooperation. At the beginning of the century, down in fact until World War II, the several disciplines existed each in a kind of splendid isolation from the others. That historians and sociologists, for example, might ever work together in curricula and research projects would have been scarcely conceivable prior to about 1945.

Each social science tended to follow the course that emerged in the 19th century: to be confined to a single, distinguishable, if artificial, area of social reality. Today, evidences are all around of cross-disciplinary work and of fusion within a single social science of elements drawn from other social sciences.

Thus there are such vital areas of work as political sociology, economic anthropology, psychology of voting, and industrial sociology. Single concepts such as "structure," "function," "alienation," and "motivation" can be seen employed variously to useful effect in several social sciences. The techniques of one social science can be seen consciously incorporated into another or into several social sciences.

If history has provided much in the way of perspective to sociology or anthropology, each of these two has provided perspective, and also whole techniques, such as statistics and survey, to history. In short, specialization is by no means without some degree at least of countertendencies such as fusion and synthesis.

Another outstanding characteristic of each of the social sciences in the 20th century is its professionalization. Without exception, the social sciences have become bodies of not merely research and teaching but also practice, in the sense that this word has in medicine or engineering. Down until about World War II, it was a rare sociologist or political scientist or anthropologist who was not a holder of academic position. There were economists and psychologists to be found in banks, industries, government, even in private consultantship, but the numbers were relatively tiny.

Overwhelmingly the social sciences had visibility alone as academic disciplines, concerned essentially with teaching and with more or less basic, individual research. All this has changed profoundly, and on a vast scale, during the past three decades. Today there are as many economists and psychologists outside academic departments as within, if not more. The number of sociologists, political scientists, and demographers to be found in government, industry, and private practice rises constantly. Equally important is the changed conception or image of the social sciences.

Today, to a degree unknown before World War II, the social sciences are conceived as policy-making disciplines, concerned with matters of national welfare in their professional capacities in just as sure a sense as any of the physical sciences. Inevitably, tensions have arisen within the social sciences as the result of processes of professionalization. Those persons who are primarily academic can all too easily feel that those who are primarily professional have different and competing identifications of themselves and their disciplines.

8.3 Criminology

This is the branch of the scientific study of the non-legal aspects of crime, including juvenile delinquency. In its wider sense, embracing penology, it is thus the study of the causation, correction, and prevention of crime--seen from the viewpoints of such diverse disciplines as ethics, anthropology, biology, ethology (the study of character), psychology and psychiatry, sociology, and statistics.

Whereas the traditional legal approach to crime focuses on the action of crime and the protection of society, criminology focuses on the person of the criminal and the essential interests of the individuals of whom society consists. Whereas criminal law has been a relatively conservative force, often slow to change even where change has seemed imperative, criminology as a part of the developing social sciences has been a revolutionary force--its object being not to replace the legal system in dealing with crime and punishment but to supplement it, making it less rigid and more sympathetic to approaches wider than strictly legal ones.

Without denying the value of "pure research," one must point to criminology and particularly penology as primarily practical subjects or "applied" disciplines. This practical value of criminological research can make itself felt in several ways. Its accumulated findings can give judges, prosecutors, lawyers, probation officers, and prison officials better understanding of crime and criminals, leading hopefully to more effective and humane sentencing and methods of treatment.

Criminological research and knowledge can be equally at the disposal of legislators and administrators to assist in their task of reforming the law and improving penal and reformatory institutions. Essentially this purveyance of information represents a neutral role for criminologists; they garner the facts, and the various governmental officials decide for themselves what kind of practical conclusions to draw from the facts.

Increasingly, however, some criminologists--like their counterparts in such fields as the atomic sciences--are demanding that scientists fully shoulder the moral and political responsibilities for their discoveries and for the use made of them instead of leaving vital decisions entirely to their governments. Thus some criminologists, for instance, insist upon actively campaigning against capital punishment, given the facts as they see them.

Opponents of this activist role, on the other hand, contend that penological arguments are not sufficient but must be weighed along with political, social, religious, and moral arguments and that this all-round consideration should be left to responsible political bodies. The view does not deny the right of criminologists to express their opinions as ordinary citizens and voters; it does contend, nevertheless, that a government of officials responsive to the popular will, however fallible it may be, is less dangerous than a "government by experts."

Another question involving the scope and functions of criminology is whether or not it should extend to the study of crime detection, involving such measures as photography, toxicology, fingerprint study, and the like. In several countries, notably Austria and Belgium, and at the school of criminology of the University of California at Berkeley, this so-called criminalistics has long been an important branch of criminological teaching and research, and the distinguished *Journal of Criminal Law, Criminology, and Police Science* (U.S.) devotes much of its space to criminal investigation. Actually, the only reason for excluding it from criminology is perhaps the expense of staff and equipment, which can be better borne by police colleges and similar specialized institutions.

On the other hand, in recent decades criminology has undergone an important and perfectly legitimate extension of its territory by devoting much attention to so-called victimology--the study of the victim of crime, his relations to the criminal, and his role as a potential causal factor in crime.

Although the exclusion of criminalistics makes it easier to locate criminology on the map of scientific studies, its origin in, its close relations to, and its partial dependence on so many other disciplines result in considerable diversity and confusion regarding its proper place in the academic curriculum. Universities in continental Europe, when they do not ignore criminology altogether, tend to treat it as part of legal education; even where its principal teachers are not lawyers.

In Great Britain the only existing Institute of Criminology is part of the law faculty of Cambridge University; in other schools criminological research and teaching are usually divided between departments of sociology or social administration, law faculties, and institutes of psychiatry. In South America the anthropological and medical elements predominate, and in the United States, criminology, with a few notable exceptions, forms an established section of departments of sociology.

Given this situation in which criminology is submerged in other fields, it is not surprising that most teachers and researchers in criminology regard themselves first as sociologists, psychologists, lawyers, or whatever and only secondarily as criminologists. Their education contributes to this status; although a number may have pursued some criminological studies in their undergraduate years, criminology is largely a postgraduate discipline, at least in terms of major concentration for students.

This floating character of criminology weakens its position and tends to lend doubt to its claim to scientific status. Nevertheless, other disciplines-- such as psychology, psychiatry, history, sociology, and social anthropology-- have gone through similar birth pangs and, even after having achieved more or less assured positions, still face challenges to their claim to being scientific disciplines.

The answer lies perhaps in historian H.R. Trevor-Roper's remark, "there are sciences and sciences." If the results of research can be viewed relatively, it is possible to perceive science in the criminologist's systematic application of sound research methods and his development of a body of facts from which he interprets general trends on a subject of real importance to mankind.

8.4 Subjectivity in the study of religion

There are, however, doubts about how far there can be neutrality and objectivity in the study of religion. Is it possible indeed to understand a faith without holding it? If it is not possible, then cross-religious comparisons would mostly break down, for normally it is not possible to be inside more than one religion. But it is necessary to be clear about what objectivity and subjectivity in religion means.

Religion can be said to be subjective in at least two senses. First, the practice of religion involves inner experiences and sentiments, such as feelings of God guiding the life of the devotee. Here religion involves subjectivity in the sense of individual experience. Religion may also be thought to be subjective because the criteria by which its truth is decided are obscure and hard to come by, so that there is no obvious "objective" test in the way in which there is for a large range of empirical claims in the physical world.

As to the first sense, one of the challenges to the student of religion is the problem of evoking its inner, individual side, which is not observable in any straightforward way. In considering a religion, however, the scholar is not only concerned with individual responses but also with communal ones. In any case, very often he is confronted only with texts describing beliefs and stories, so that he needs to infer the inner sentiments that these both evoke and express.

The adherent of a faith is no doubt authoritative as to his own experience, but he is not necessarily so in regard to the communal significance of the rites and institutions in which he participates. Thus, the matter of coming to understand the inner side of a religion involves dialectic between participant observation and dialogical (interpersonal) relationship with the adherents of the other faith. Consequently, the study of religion has strong similarities to, and indeed overlaps with, anthropology.

General agreement upon scholarly methods, however, does not exist, partly because different scholars have come to the study of religion from different disciplines and points of view--such as history, theology, philosophy of religion, and sociology.

The other sense of the subjectivity of religion is properly a matter for philosophy of religion and theology (Christian and otherwise). The study of religion can roughly be divided between descriptive and historical inquiries, on the one hand, and normative inquiries, on the other. The latter primarily concern the truth of religious claims, the acceptability of religious values, and other such normative aspects; the former, only indirectly involved with the normative elements of religion, are primarily concerned with its history, structure, and similar descriptive elements.

The distinction, however, is not an absolute one, for, as has been noted, descriptions of religion may sometimes incorporate theories about religion that imply something about the truth or other normative aspects of some or all religions. Conversely, theological claims may imply something about the history of a religion. The dominant sense in which one speaks nowadays of the study of religion is the descriptive sense.

8.5 Application of ergonomics

Ergonomics or human engineering is the science dealing with the application of information on physical and psychological characteristics to the design of devices and systems for human use.

The term human-factors engineering is used to designate equally a body of knowledge, a process, and a profession. As a body of knowledge, human-factors engineering is a collection of data and principles about human characteristics, capabilities, and limitations in relation to machines, jobs, and environments.

As a process, it refers to the design of machines, machine systems, work methods, and environments to take into account the safety, comfort, and productiveness of human users and operators. As a profession, human-factors engineering includes a range of scientists and engineers from several disciplines that are concerned with individuals and small groups at work.

8.6 Human factors

The terms human-factors engineering and human engineering are used interchangeably on the North American continent. In Europe, Japan, and most of the rest of the world the prevalent term is ergonomics, a word made up of the Greek words, *ergon*, meaning "work," and *nomos*, meaning "law." Despite minor differences in emphasis, the terms human-factors engineering and ergonomics may be considered synonymous.

Human factors and human engineering were used in the 1920s and '30s to refer to problems of human relations in industry, an older connotation that has gradually dropped out of use. Some small specialized groups prefer such labels as bioastronautics, bio-dynamics, bioengineering, and manned-systems technology; these represent special emphases whose differences are much smaller than the similarities in their aims and goals.

The data and principles of human-factors engineering are concerned with human performance, behaviour, and training in man-machine systems; the design and development of man-machine systems; and systems-related biological or medical research. Because of its broad scope, human-factors engineering draws upon parts of such social or physiological sciences as anatomy, anthropometry, applied physiology, environmental medicine, psychology, sociology, and toxicology, as well as parts of engineering, industrial design, and operations research.

8.7 Comparative ethics

This is the empirical (observational) study of the moral beliefs and practices of different peoples and cultures in various places and times. It aims not only to elaborate such beliefs and practices but also to understand them insofar as they are causally conditioned by social, economic, and geographic circumstances. Comparative ethics, in contrast to normative ethics, is thus the proper subject matter of the social sciences (*e.g.*, anthropology, history, sociology, and psychology).

Empirical studies show that all societies have moral rules that prescribe or forbid certain classes of action and that these rules are accompanied by sanctions to ensure their enforcement. Of particular interest in comparative ethics are the similarities and differences between the moral practices and beliefs of different people, as explained by physical and economic conditions, opportunities for cross-cultural contacts, and the force of inherited traditions facing new social or technological challenges.

It has been observed, for example, that virtually every society has well-established norms dealing with such matters as family organization and individual duties, sexual activity, property rights, personal welfare, truth telling, and promise keeping, but not all societies have evolved the same norms for these various aspects of human conduct.

Some social scientists concentrate their attention on the universality of basic moral rules, such as those forbidding murder, theft, infidelity, and incest. Others are more concerned with the diversity of moral practices--*e.g.*, monogamy versus polygamy; caring for the aged versus parricide; the forbidding of abortion versus voluntary feticide. The question then arises whether similarity or diversity is more fundamental, whether similarity supports the validity of the practice, and whether diversity supports a relativism and scepticism.

Clearly a consensus of all peoples in a moral opinion does not of itself establish validity. On the other hand, widespread agreement may support the argument that morality is rooted in human nature, and, if human nature is fundamentally everywhere the same, it will also manifest this similarity in significant ways, including morality. Such questions are philosophical and lie beyond the scope of the social sciences, which are restricted to empirically verifiable generalizations.

Another question concerns the development of morals. Insofar as this is an empirical issue, it must be distinguished from the question whether there is progress in morality. For progress is an evaluative term--whether the moral ideals, for example, or the practices of civilized peoples, or both, are higher than those of primitive peoples is itself a question of moral judgment rather than of social science. Still, social scientists and moral philosophers alike have noted important changes that have taken place in the historical development of various peoples.

8.8 Influence of science

What separates modern criticism from earlier work is its catholicity of scope and method, its borrowing of procedures from the social sciences, and its unprecedented attention to detail. As literature's place in society has become more problematic and peripheral, and as humanistic education has grown into a virtual industry with a large group of professionals serving as one another's judges, criticism has evolved into a complex discipline, increasingly refined in its procedures but often lacking a sense of contact with the general social will.

Major modern critics, to be sure, have not allowed their "close reading" to distract them from certain perennial questions about poetic truth, the nature of literary satisfaction, and literature's social utility, but even these matters have sometimes been cast in "value-free" empirical terms.

Recourse to scientific authority and method, then, is the outstanding trait of 20th-century criticism. The sociology of Marx, Max Weber, and Karl Mannheim, the mythological investigations of Sir James George Frazer and his followers, Edmund Husserl's phenomenology, Claude Levi-Strauss's anthropological structuralism, and the psychological models proposed by Sigmund Freud and C.G. Jung have all found their way into criticism.

The result has been not simply an abundance of technical terms and rules, but a widespread belief that literature's governing principles can be located outside literature. Jungian "archetypal" criticism, for example, regularly identifies literary power with the presence of certain themes that are alleged to inhabit the myths and beliefs of all cultures, while psychoanalytic exegetes interpret poems in exactly the manner that Freud interpreted dreams. Such procedures may encourage the critic, wisely or unwisely, to discount traditional boundaries between genres, national literatures, and levels of culture; the critical enterprise begins to seem continuous with a general study of man.

The impetus toward universalism can be discerned even in those critics, who are most sceptical of it, the so-called historical relativists who attempt to reconstruct each epoch's outlook and to understand works as they appeared to their first readers. Historical relativism does undermine cross-cultural notions of beauty, but it reduces the record of any given period to data from which inferences can be systematically drawn. Here, too, in other words, uniform methodology tends to replace the intuitive connoisseurship that formerly typified the critic's sense of his role.

8.9 Christian influences

Others have sought to construct theologies in the mold of 19th-century German idealism (*e.g.,* Paul Tillich); some, as process theologians, in that of the early 20th-century British mathematician and metaphysician Alfred North Whitehead (*e.g.,* Charles Hartshorne on the doctrine of God, John Cobb on Christology); some, the liberation theologians, in highly pragmatic and political terms (*e.g.,* Juan Luis Segundo, Gustavo Gutiérrez); and some, as feminist theologians, in terms of the newly awakened self-consciousness of women and the awareness of a distorting patriarchial influence on all past forms of Christian thought (*e.g.,* Rosemary Ruether, Elizabeth Fiorenza).

Most theologians, however, have continued to accept the traditional structure of Christian beliefs. The more liberal among them have sought to detach these from the older conceptualities and to reformulate them so as to connect with modern consciousness (*e.g.,* Friedrich Schleiermacher, Albrecht Ritschl, Adolf von Harnack, Karl Rahner, Gordon Kaufman); while the more conservative have sought to defend the traditional formulations within an increasingly alien intellectual environment (*e.g.,* B.B. Warfield, Charles Hodge, Karl Barth, Cornelis Berkouwer).

Of the factors forming the intellectual environment of Christian thought in the modern period, perhaps the most powerful have been the physical and human sciences. The former have compelled the rethinking of certain Christian doctrines, as astronomy undermined the assumption of the centrality of the Earth in the universe, as geologic evidence concerning its age rendered implausible the biblical chronology, and as biology located humanity within the larger evolution of the forms of life on Earth.

The human sciences of anthropology, psychology, sociology, and historical research have suggested possible naturalistic explanations of religion itself based, for example, upon the projection of desire for a cosmic father figure, the need for socially cohesive symbols, or the power of royal and priestly classes. Such naturalistic interpretations of religion, together with the ever-widening scientific understanding of the physical universe, have prompted some Christian philosophers to think of the religious ambiguity of the universe as a totality that can, from the human standpoint within it, be interpreted in both naturalistic and religious ways, thus providing scope for the exercise of faith as a free response to the mystery of existence.

9. SOCIAL SCIENCES AND RELATED SUBJECTS

9.1 Development of the separate disciplines

Among the disciplines that formed the social sciences, two contrary, for a time equally powerful, tendencies at first dominated them. The first was the drive toward unification, toward a single, master social science, whatever it might be called. The second tendency was toward specialization of the individual social sciences. If, clearly, it is the second that has triumphed, with the results to be seen in the disparate, sometimes jealous, highly specialized disciplines seen today, the first was not without great importance and must also be examined.

What emerges from the critical rationalism of the 18th century is not, in the first instance, a conception of need for a plurality of social sciences, but rather for a single science of society that would take its place in the hierarchy of the sciences that included the fields of astronomy, physics, chemistry, and biology. When, in the 1820s, Comte wrote calling for a new science, one with man the social animal as the subject, he assuredly had but a single, encompassing science of society in mind--not a congeries of disciplines, each concerned with some single aspect of man's behaviour in society. The same was true of Bentham, Marx, and Spencer.

All these minds, and there were many others to join them, saw the study of society as a unified enterprise. They would have scoffed, and on occasion did, at any notion of a separate economics, political science, sociology, and so on. Society is an indivisible thing, they would have argued; so, too, must be the study of society.

It was, however, the opposite tendency of specialization or differentiation that won out. No matter how the century began, or what were the dreams of a Comte, Spencer, or Marx, when the 19th century ended, not one but several distinct, competitive social sciences were to be found. Aiding this process was the development of the colleges and universities. With hindsight it might be said that the cause of universities in the future would have been strengthened, as would the cause of the social sciences, had there come into existence, successfully, a single curriculum, undifferentiated by field, for the study of society. What in fact happened, however, was the opposite.

The growing desire for an elective system, for a substantial number of academic specializations, and for differentiation of academic degrees, contributed strongly to the differentiation of the social sciences. This was first and most strongly to be seen in Germany, where, from about 1815 on, all scholarship and science were based in the universities and where competition for status among the several disciplines was keen.

But by the end of the century the same phenomenon of specialization was to be found in the United States (where admiration for the German system was very great in academic circles) and, in somewhat less degree, in France and England. Admittedly, the differentiation of the social sciences in the 19th century was but one aspect of a larger process that was to be seen as vividly in the physical sciences and the humanities. No major field escaped the lure of specialization of investigation, and clearly, a great deal of the sheer bulk of learning that passed from the 19th to the 20th century was the direct consequence of this specialization.

9.2 Intellect and philosophy

It is important also to identify three other powerful tendencies of thought that influenced all of the social sciences. The first is a positivism that was not merely an appeal to science but almost reverence for science; the second, humanitarianism; the third, the philosophy of evolution.

The Positivist appeal of science was to be seen everywhere. The rise of the ideal of science in the Age of Reason was noted above. The 19th century saw the virtual institutionalization of this ideal--possibly even canonization. The great aim was that of dealing with moral values, institutions, and all social phenomena through the same fundamental methods that could be seen so luminously in such areas as physics and biology.

Prior to the 19th century, no very clear distinction had been made between philosophy and science, and the term philosophy was even preferred by those working directly with physical materials, seeking laws and principles in the fashion of a Newton or Harvey--that is, by persons whom one would now call scientists.

In the 19th century, in contrast, the distinction between philosophy and science became an overwhelming one. Virtually every area of man's thought and behaviour was thought by a rising number of persons to be amenable to scientific investigation in precisely the same degree that physical data were. More than anyone else, it was Comte who heralded the idea of the scientific treatment of social behaviour. His *Cours de philosophie positive*, published in six volumes between 1830 and 1842, sought to demonstrate irrefutably not merely the possibility but the inevitability of a science of man, one for which Comte coined the word "sociology" and that would do for man the social being exactly what biology had already done for man the biological animal. But Comte was far from alone. There were many in the century to join in his celebration of science for the study of society.

9.3 Humanitarianism

Humanitarianism, though a very distinguishable current of thought in the century, was closely related to the idea of a science of society. For the ultimate purpose of social science was thought by almost everyone to be the welfare of society, the improvement of its moral and social condition. Humanitarianism, strictly defined, is the institutionalization of compassion; it is the extension of welfare and succour from the limited areas in which these had historically been found, chiefly family and village, to society at large.

One of the most notable and also distinctive aspects of the 19th century was the constantly rising number of persons, almost wholly from the middle class, who worked directly for the betterment of society. In the many projects and proposals for relief of the destitute, improvement of slums, amelioration of the plight of the insane, the indigent, and imprisoned, and other afflicted minorities could be seen the spirit of humanitarianism at work.

All kinds of associations were formed, including temperance associations, groups and societies for the abolition of slavery and of poverty and for the improvement of literacy, among other objectives. Nothing like the 19th-century spirit of humanitarianism had ever been seen before in Western Europe--not even in France during the Enlightenment, where interest in mankind's salvation tended to be more intellectual than humanitarian in the strict sense. Humanitarianism and social science were reciprocally related in their purposes. All that helped the cause of the one could be seen as helpful to the other.

The third of the intellectual influences is that of evolution. It affected every one of the social sciences, each of which was as much concerned with the development of things as with their structures. An interest in development was to be found in the 18th century, as noted earlier. But this interest was small and specialized compared with 19th-century theories of social evolution. The impact of Charles Darwin's *Origin of Species*, published in 1859, was of course great and further enhanced the appeal of the evolutionary view of things. But it is very important to recognize that ideas of social evolution had their own origins and contexts.

The evolutionary works of such social scientists as Comte, Herbert Spencer, and Marx had been completed, or well begun, before publication of Darwin's work. The important point, in any event, is that the idea or the philosophy of evolution was in the air throughout the century, as profoundly contributory to the establishment of sociology as a systematic discipline in the 1830s as to such fields as geology, astronomy, and biology. Evolution was as permeative an idea as the Trinity had been in medieval Europe.

9.4 Neutrality in the study of religion

The attempt to be descriptive about religious beliefs and practices, without judging them to be valuable or otherwise, is often considered to involve *epoche*--that is, the suspension of belief and the "bracketing" of the phenomena under investigation. The idea of *epoche* is borrowed from the philosophy of the German thinker Edmund Husserl (1859-1938), the father of Phenomenology, and the procedure is regarded as central to the phenomenology of religion.

In this context the term phenomenology refers first to the attempt to describe religious phenomena in a way that brings out the beliefs and attitudes of the adherents of the religion under investigation, but without either endorsing or rejecting these beliefs and attitudes. Thus, the bracketing means forgetting about one's own beliefs that might endorse or conflict with what is being investigated. Second, phenomenology of religion refers to the attempt to devise a typology of religious phenomena--to classify religious activities, beliefs, and institutions.

To some extent the emphasis on neutral description arises in modern times as a reaction against "committed" accounts of religion, which were for long the norm and still exist where religion is treated from a theological point of view. The Christian theologian, for example, may see a particular historical process as providential or as providing significance for Christian living. This is a legitimate perspective from the standpoint of faith. But the historical process itself has to be investigated in the first instance "scientifically"--that is, by considering the evidence, using the techniques of historical enquiry and other scientific methods. Conflict sometimes arises because the committed point of view is likely to begin from a more conservative stance--*i.e.*, to accept at face value the scriptural accounts of events--whereas the "secular" historian may be more sceptical, especially of records of miraculous events. The study of religion may thus come to have a reflexive effect on religion itself, such as the manner in which modern Christian theology has been profoundly affected by the whole question of the historicity of the New Testament.

The reflexive effect of the study of religion on religion itself may in practice make it more difficult for the student of religion to adopt the detachment implied by bracketing. Scholars generally agree, however, that the pursuit of objectivity is desirable, provided this does not involve sacrificing a sense of the inner aspect of religion. Thus, the stress on the distinction between the descriptive and normative approaches is becoming more frequent among scholars of religion.

The study of religion may thus be characterized as concerned with man's religious behaviour in relation to the transcendent, to God or the gods, and whatever else is regarded as sacred or holy, and as a study that attempts to be faithful both to the outer and inner facts. Its present-day concern is predominantly descriptive and explanatory and hence embraces such various disciplines as history, sociology, anthropology, psychology, and archaeology.

Traditionally, however, the study has been more oriented toward truth claims in religion--these being properly the concern of theology and philosophy of religion. Needless to say, there are different sorts of theology, related to the different religious traditions, such as Christian, Muslim, and Buddhist. But insofar as the theologian expresses and articulates a tradition, he belongs to it and thus is part of the subject matter studied by the student of religion.

9.5 Christian community and the world

From the perspectives of history and sociology, the Christian community has been related to the world in diverse and even paradoxical ways. This is reflected not only in changes in this relationship over time but also in simultaneously expressed alternatives ranging from withdrawal from and rejection of the world to theocratic triumphalism. For example, early Christians so consistently rejected imperial deities that they were known as radical atheists, while later Christians so embraced European monarchies that they were known as reactionary theists.

Radical medieval Franciscans proclaimed that true Christians should divest themselves of money at the same time that the papacy expended great sums to manipulate the political landscape of Europe. Another classic example of this paradoxical relationship is the early monastic withdrawal from the world that at the same time preserved and transmitted classical culture and learning to medieval Europe.

In the modern period some Christian communities regard secularization as a fall from true Christianity; others view it as a legitimate consequence of a desacralization of the world initiated by Christ.

The Christian community is always part of the world in which it exists. Thus, the church has served the typical religious function of legitimating social systems and values and of creating structures of meaning, plausibility, and compensation for society as it faces loss and death. The Christian community has sometimes exercised this religious function in collusion with tribalistic nationalisms (*e.g.*, the "German Christians" and Nazism) by disregarding traditional church tenets.

When the Christian community has held to its teachings, however, it has opposed such social systems and values (*e.g.*, the stance of the Confessing Church of Germany against Nazism). Given the inherent fragility of human culture and society, religion in general and the Christian community in particular frequently are conservative forces.

However, the Christian community is not always a conservative force. Its ability to criticize the world was bitterly acknowledged by those Romans who attributed the fall of their empire to Christian undermining of their "civil religion." Contemporary black theology and Latin-American liberation theology share the conviction that God takes the side of the oppressed against the world's injustices.

From the perspective of theology or faith, the criticism of the world of which the Christian community itself is a part is the exercise of its commitment to Jesus Christ. For the Christian community, the death and Resurrection of Jesus call into question all structures, systems, and values of the world that claim ultimacy.

The relationship of the Christian community to the world may be seen differently depending upon one's historical, sociological, and theological perspectives because the Christian community is both a creation in the world and an influence upon it. This complexity led the American theologian H. Richard Niebuhr to comment in *Christ and Culture* (1956) that "the many-sided debate about the relations of Christianity and civilization . . . is as confused as it is many-sided."

9.6 Ethical relativism

This is the view that what is right or wrong and good or bad is not absolute but variable and relative, depending on the person, circumstances, or social situation. The view is as ancient as Protagoras, a leading Greek Sophist of the 5th century BC, and as modern as the scientific approaches of sociology and anthropology.

Many people's understanding of this view is often vague and confused. It is not simply the belief, for example, that what is right depends on the circumstances, because everyone, including the absolutists, agrees that circumstances can make a difference; it is acknowledged that whether it is right for a man to enter a certain house depends upon whether he is the owner, a guest, a police officer with a warrant, or a burglar. Nor is it the belief that what someone thinks is right is relative to his social conditioning, for again anyone can agree that there are causal influences behind what people think is right.

Ethical relativism is, rather, the view that what is really right depends solely upon what the individual or the society thinks is right. Because what one thinks will vary with time and place, what is right will also vary accordingly. Ethical relativism is, therefore, a view about the truth status of moral principles, according to which changing and even conflicting moral principles are equally true, so that there is no objective way of justifying any principle as valid for all people and all societies.

The sociological argument for relativism proceeds from the diversity of different cultures. Ruth Benedict, an American anthropologist, suggested, for example, in *Patterns of Culture* (1934) that the differing and even conflicting moral beliefs and behaviour of the North American Indian Kwakiutl, Pueblo, and Dobu cultures provided standards that were sufficient within each culture for its members to evaluate correctly their own individual actions. Thus, relativism does not deprive one of all moral guidance.

However, some anthropologists, such as Clyde Kluckhohn and Ralph Linton, have pointed up certain "ethical universals," or cross-cultural similarities, in moral beliefs and practices--such as prohibitions against murder, incest, untruth, and unfair dealing--that are more impressive than the particularities of moral disagreement, which can be interpreted as arising within the more basic framework that the universals provide. Some critics point out, further, that a relativist has no grounds by which to evaluate the social criticism arising within a free or open society, that his view appears in fact to undercut the very idea of social reform.

A second argument for relativism is that of the skeptic who holds that moral utterances are not cognitive statements, verifiable as true or false, but are, instead, emotional expressions of approval or disapproval or are merely prescriptions for action. In this view, variations and conflicts between moral utterances are relative to the varying conditions that occasion such feelings, attitudes, or prescriptions, and there is nothing more to be said.

Critics of the sceptical view may observe that classifying moral utterances as emotive expressions does not in itself disqualify them from functioning simultaneously as beliefs with cognitive content. Or again, they may observe that, even if moral utterances are not cognitive, it does not follow that they are related, as the relativist suggests, only to the changeable elements in their background; they may also be related in a special way to needs and wants that are common and essential to human nature and society everywhere and in every age.

If so, the criticism continues, these needs can provide good reasons for the justification of some moral utterances over others. The relativist will then have to reply either that human nature has no such common, enduring needs or that, if it does, they cannot be discovered and employed to ground man's moral discourse.

9.7 Applications of logic and mathematics

Despite the numerous types of communication or information theory extant today--and those likely to be formulated tomorrow--the most rationally and experimentally consistent approaches to communication theory so far developed follow the constructions of Shannon and others described above. Such approaches tend to employ the structural rigours of logic rather than the looser syntaxes, grammars, and vocabularies of common languages, with their symbolic, poetic, and inferential aspects of meaning.

Cybernetic theory and computer technology require rigorous but straightforward languages to permit translation into nonambiguous, special symbols that can be stored and utilized for statistical manipulations. The closed system of formal logic proved ideal for this need. Premises and conclusions drawn from syllogisms according to logical rules may be easily tested in a consistent, scientific manner, as long as all parties communicating share the rational premises employed by the particular system.

That this logical mode of communication drew its frame of discourse from the logic of the ancient Greeks was inevitable. Translated into an Aristotelian manner of discourse, meaningful interactions between individuals could be transferred to an equally rational closed system of mathematics: an arithmetic for simple transactions, an algebra for solving certain well-delimited puzzles, a calculus to simulate changes, rates and flows, and a geometry for purposes of illustration and model construction.

This progression has proved quite useful for handling those limited classes of communications that arise out of certain structured, rational operations, like those in economics, inductively oriented sociology, experimental psychology, and other behavioral and social sciences, as well as in most of the natural sciences.

The basic theorem of information theory rests, first, upon the assumption that the message transmitted is well organized, consistent, and characterized by relatively low and determinable degrees of entropy and redundancy. (Otherwise, the mathematical structure might yield only probability statements approaching random scatters, of little use to anyone.)

Under these circumstances, by devising proper coding procedures for the transmitter, it becomes possible to transmit symbols over a channel at an average rate that is nearly the capacity of units per second of the channel (symbolized by C) as a function of the units per second from an information source (H)--but never at rates in excess of capacity divided by units per second (C/H), no matter how expertly the symbols are coded.

As simple as this notion seems, upon determining the capacity of the channel and by cleverly coding the information involved, precise mathematical models of information transactions (similar to electronic frequencies of energy transmissions) may be evolved and employed for complex analyses within the strictures of formal logic. They must, of course, take into account as precisely as possible levels of entropy and redundancy as well as other known variables.

The internal capacities of the channel studied and the sophistication of the coding procedures that handle the information limit the usefulness of the theorem presented above. At present such procedures, while they may theoretically offer broad prospects, are restricted by formal encoding procedures that depend upon the capacities of the instruments in which they are stored (nowadays, mostly on magnetic tape and disk-packs in computers).

Although such devices can handle quickly the logic of vast amounts of relatively simple information, they cannot match the flexibility and complexity of the human brain, still man's prime instrument for managing the subtleties of most communication.

9.8 Oligarchy

Political science and sociology are beginning to differentiate more carefully between various types of control and power. The type of power held by a Democratic Party boss, while overwhelming in relation to any single member of the party, is very different from that wielded by the boss of the single party in a totalitarian and authoritarian pattern.

Likewise, the control group within an organization does not occupy the same position under democratic conditions (which provide for the group's being effectively challenged by outsiders at any time) as it does under an authoritarian plan. If effective control changes hands as rapidly as it does in a city of the United States or a British trade union, it is doubtful that those exercising it should be spoken of as a "class" or an "elite."

The expression "the few" is too abstract to convey much information. Like the other purely numerical concepts of government inherited from Greek philosophy, oligarchy is an outmoded term, because it fails to direct attention to the substantive features of a government. This refers to government by the few, especially despotic power exercised by a small and privileged group for corrupt or selfish purposes.

Aristotle used the term *oligarchia* to designate the rule of the few when it was exercised not by the best but by bad men unjustly. In this sense, oligarchy is a debased form of aristocracy, which denotes government by the few in which power is vested in the best individuals.

Most classic oligarchies have resulted when governing elites were recruited exclusively from a ruling caste--a hereditary social grouping that is set apart from the rest of society by religion, kinship, economic status, prestige, or even language. Such elites tend to exercise power in the interests of their own class.

It is a recurrent idea that all forms of government are in the final analysis reducible to the rule of a few. Oligarchs will secure effective control whether the formal authority is vested in the people, a monarch, the proletariat, or a dictator. Thus, Karl Marx and Friedrich Engels insisted that, throughout capitalism, the key capitalists had controlled the government; they coined the dictum, "the state is the executive committee of the exploiting class."

The Italian political scientist Gaetano Mosca likewise insisted that a "ruling class" always constituted the effective oligarchic control. Vilfredo Pareto elaborated the idea in his doctrine of the "elite." The modern tendency to analyze social patterns in terms of an "elite," although greatly reinforced by Pareto's theory, goes further back than Marx and Engels, who employed the term "elite" to describe the class-conscious communists, the leading group within the proletariat.

One of the most famous modern uses of the term occurs in "iron law of oligarchy," a concept devised by the German sociologist Robert Michels to refer to the alleged inevitable tendency of political parties and trade unions to become bureaucratized, centralized, and conservative. His reasoning was that, no matter how egalitarian or even radical the original ideology and goals of a party or union may be, there must emerge a limited group of leaders at the centre who can direct power efficiently, get things done through an administrative staff, and evolve some kind of rigorous order and ideology to ensure the survival of the organization when faced by internal division and external opposition.

Subsequent writers of various persuasions have attempted either to expand on Michel's thesis, extending it to legislatures, religious orders, and other organizations, or to restrict or criticize the thesis, charging that the iron law of oligarchy is not universal and that some unions and parties do maintain a viable system of democratic expression and governance.

9.9 Nature of the research

The emphasis upon research in the social sciences has become almost transcending within recent decades. This situation is not at all different from that which prevails in the physical sciences and the professions in this age. Prior to about 1945, the functions of teaching and research had approximately equal value in many universities and colleges.

The idea of a social (or physical) scientist appointed to an academic institution for research alone, or with research preponderant, was scarcely known. Research bureaus and institutes in the social sciences were very few and did not rival traditional academic departments and colleges as prestige-bearing entities. All of that was changed decisively beginning with the period just after World War II.

From governments and foundations, large sums of money passed into the universities--usually not to the universities as such, but rather to individuals or small groups of individuals, each eminent for research. Research became the uppermost value in the social sciences (as in the physical) and hence, of course, in the universities themselves.

Probably the greatest single change in the social sciences during the past generation has been the widespread introduction of mathematical and other quantitative methods. Without question, economics is the discipline in which the most spectacular changes of this kind have taken place.

So great is the dominance of mathematical techniques here--resulting in the eruption of what is called econometrics to a commanding position in the discipline--that, to the outsider, economics today almost appears to be a branch of mathematics. But in sociology, political science, social psychology, and anthropology, the impact of quantitative methods, above all, of statistics, has also been notable. No longer does statistics stand alone, a separate discipline, as it did in effect during the 19th century.

This area today is inseparable from each of the social sciences, though, in the field of mathematics, statistics still remains eminently distinguishable, the focus of highly specialized research and theory.

Within the past decade or two, the use of computers and of all the complex techniques associated with computers has become a staple of social-science research and teaching. Through the data storage and data retrieval of electronic computers, working with amounts and diversity of data that would call for the combined efforts of hundreds, even thousands of technicians, the social sciences have been able to deal with both the extensive and intensive aspects of human behaviour in ways that would once have been inconceivable.

The so-called computer revolution in modern thought has been, in short, as vivid a phase of the social as the physical sciences, not to mention other areas of modern life. The problem as it is stated by mature social scientists is to use computers in ways in which they are best fitted but without falling into the fallacy that they can alone guide, direct, and supply vital perspective in the study of man.

Closely related to mathematical, computer, and other quantitative aspects of the social sciences is the vast increase in the empiricism of modern social science. Never in history has so much in the way of data been collected, examined, classified, and brought to the uses of social theory and social policy alike. What has been called the triumph of the fact is nowhere more visible than in the social sciences.

Without question, this massive empiricism has been valuable, indispensable indeed, to those seeking explanations of social structures and processes. Empiricism, however, like quantitative method, is not enough in itself. Unless related to hypothesis, theory, or conclusion, it is sterile, and most of the leading social scientists of today reflect this view in their works. Too many, however, deal with the gathering and classifying of data as though these were themselves sufficient.

It is the quest for data, for detailed, factual knowledge of human beliefs, opinions, and attitudes, as well as patterns and styles of life--familial, occupational, political, religious, and so on--that has made the use of surveys and polls another of the major tendencies in the social sciences of this century. The poll data one sees in his newspaper are hardly more than the exposed portion of an iceberg. Literally thousands of polls, questionnaires, and surveys are going on at any given moment today in the social sciences. The survey or polling method ranks with the quantitative indeed in popularity in the social sciences, both being, obviously, indispensable tools of the empiricism just mentioned.

9.10 Democratic and industrial change

It is illuminating to mention a few of the major themes in social thought in the 19th century that were almost the direct results of the democratic and industrial revolutions. It should be borne in mind that these themes are to be seen in the philosophical and literary writing of the age as well as in social thought.

First, there was the great increase in population. Between 1750 and 1850 the population of Europe went from 140,000,000 to 266,000,000; in the world from 728,000,000 to well over 1,000,000,000. It was an English clergyman-economist, Thomas Malthus, who, in his famous *Essay on Population*, first marked the enormous significance to human welfare of this increase.

With the diminution of historic checks on population growth, chiefly those of high mortality rates--a diminution that was, as Malthus realized, one of the rewards of technical progress--there were no easily foreseeable limits to growth of population. And such growth, he stressed, could only upset the traditional balance between population, which Malthus described as growing at geometrical rate, and food supply, which he declared could grow only at arithmetical rate. Not all social scientists in the century took the pessimistic view of the matter that Malthus did but few if any were indifferent to the impact of explosive increase in population on economy, government, and society.

Second, there was the condition of labour. It may be possible to see this condition in the early 19th century as in fact better than the condition of the rural masses at earlier times. But the important point is that to a large number of writers in the 19th century it seemed worse and was defined as worse.

The wrenching of large numbers of people from the older and protective contexts of village, guild, parish, and family, and their massing in the new centres of industry, forming slums, living in common squalor and wretchedness, their wages generally behind cost of living, their families growing larger, their standard of living becoming lower, as it seemed--all of this is a frequent theme in the social thought of the century.

Economics indeed became known as the "dismal science," because economists, from David Ricardo to Karl Marx, could see little likelihood of the condition of labour improving under capitalism.

Third, there was the transformation of property. Not only was more and more property to be seen as industrial--manifest in the factories, business houses, and workshops of the period--but also the very nature of property was changing. Whereas for most of the history of mankind property had been "hard," visible only in concrete possessions--land and money--now the more intangible kinds of property such as shares of stock, negotiable equities of all kinds, and bonds were assuming ever greater influence in the economy.

This led, as was early realized, to the dominance of financial interests, to speculation, and to a general widening of the gulf between the propertied and the masses.

The change in the character of property made easier the concentration of property, the accumulation of immense wealth in the hands of a relative few, and, not least, the possibility of economic domination of politics and culture. It should not be thought that only socialists saw property in this light. From Edmund Burke through Auguste Comte, Frédéric Le Play, and John Stuart Mill down to Karl Marx, Max Weber, and Émile Durkheim, one finds conservatives and liberals looking at the impact of this change in analogous ways.

Fourth, there was urbanization--the sudden increase in the number of towns and cities in Western Europe and the increase in number of persons living in the historic towns and cities. Whereas in earlier centuries, the city had been regarded almost uniformly as a setting of civilization, culture, and freedom of mind, now one found more and more writers aware of the other side of cities: the atomization of human relationships, broken families, the sense of the mass, of anonymity, alienation, and disrupted values. Sociology particularly among the social sciences turned its attention to the problems of urbanization.

The contrast between the more organic type of community found in rural areas and the more mechanical and individualistic society of the cities is a basic contrast in sociology, one that was given much attention by such pioneers in Europe as the French sociologists Frédéric Le Play and Émile Durkheim; the German sociologists Ferdinand Tönnies, Georg Simmel, and Max Weber; the Belgian statistician Adolphe Quetelet; and, in America, by the sociologists Charles H. Cooley and Robert E. Park.

Fifth, there was technology. With the spread of mechanization, first in the factories, then in agriculture, social thinkers could see possibilities of a rupture of the historic relation between man and nature, between man and man, even between man and God. To thinkers as politically different as Thomas Carlyle and Karl Marx, technology seemed to lead to dehumanization of the worker and to exercise of a new kind of tyranny over human life.

Marx, though, far from despising technology, thought the advent of socialism would counteract all this. Alexis de Tocqueville declared that technology, and especially technical specialization of work, was more degrading to man's mind and spirit than even political tyranny.

It was thus in the 19th century that the opposition to technology on moral, psychological, and aesthetic grounds first made its appearance in Western thought.

Sixth, there was the factory system. The importance of this to 19th-century thought has been intimated above. Suffice it to add that along with urbanization and spreading mechanization, the system of work whereby masses of workers left home and family to work long hours in the factories became a major theme of social thought as well as of social reform.

Seventh, and finally, mention is to be made of the development of political masses--that is, the slow but inexorable widening of franchise and electorate through which ever larger numbers of persons became aware of themselves as voters and participants in the political process.

This too is a major theme in social thought, to be seen most luminously perhaps in Tocqueville's *Democracy in America*, a classic written in the 1830s that took not merely America but democracy everywhere as its subject. Tocqueville saw the rise of the political masses, more especially the immense power that could be wielded by the masses, as the single greatest threat to individual freedom and cultural diversity in the ages ahead.

These, then, are the principal themes in the 19th-century writing that may be seen as direct results of the two great revolutions. As themes, they are to be found not only in the social sciences but, as noted above, in a great deal of the philosophical and literary writing of the century. In their respective ways, the philosophers Hegel, Coleridge, and Emerson were as struck by the consequences of the revolutions as were any social scientists. So too were such novelists as Balzac and Dickens.

10. ANTHROPOLOGY AND ETHICS

10.1 Cultural variations

It is commonly believed that there are no ethical universals--*i.e.*, there is so much variation from one culture to another that no single principle or judgment is generally accepted. We have already seen that such is not the case. Of course, there are immense differences in the way in which the broad principles so far discussed are applied.

The duty of children to their parents meant one thing in traditional Chinese society and means something quite different in contemporary Anglo-Saxon society. Yet, concern for kin and reciprocity to those who treat us well are considered good in virtually all human societies. Also, all societies have, for obvious reasons, some constraints on killing and wounding other members of the group.

Beyond that common ground, the variations in moral attitudes soon become more striking than the similarities. Man's fascination with such variations goes back a long way. The Greek historian Herodotus relates that Darius, king of Persia, once summoned Greeks before him and asked them how much he would have to pay them to eat their fathers' dead bodies.

They refused to do it at any price. Then Darius brought in some Indians who by custom ate the bodies of their parents and asked them what would make them willing to burn their fathers' bodies. The Indians cried out that he should not mention so horrid an act. Herodotus drew the obvious moral: each nation thinks its own customs best.

Variations in morals were not systematically studied until the 19th century, when knowledge of the more remote parts of the globe began to increase. At the beginning of the 20th century, Edward Westermarck published *The Origin and Development of the Moral Ideas* (1906-08), two large volumes comparing differences among societies in such matters as the wrongness of killing (including killing in warfare, euthanasia, suicide, infanticide, abortion, human sacrifices, and duelling); whose duty it is to support children, the aged, or the poor; the forms of sexual relationship permitted; the status of women; the right to property and what constitutes theft; the holding of slaves; the duty to tell the truth; dietary restrictions; concern for nonhuman animals; duties to the dead; and duties to the gods.

Westermarck had no difficulty in demonstrating tremendous diversity in all these issues. More recent, though less comprehensive, studies have confirmed that human societies can and do flourish while holding radically different views about all such matters.

As noted earlier, ethics itself is not primarily concerned with the description of moral systems in different societies. That task, which remains on the level of description, is one for anthropology or sociology. In contrast, ethics deals with the justification of moral principles.

Nevertheless, ethics must take note of the variations in moral systems because it has often been claimed that this knowledge shows that morality is simply a matter of what is customary and is always relative to a particular society.

According to this view, no ethical principles can be valid except in terms of the society in which they are held. Words such as good and bad just mean, it is claimed, "approved in my society" or "disapproved in my society," and so to search for an objective, or rationally justifiable, ethic is to search for what is in fact an illusion.

One way of replying to this position would be to stress the fact that there are some features common to virtually all human moralities. It might be thought that these common features must be the universally valid and objective core of morality. This argument would, however, involve a fallacy. If the explanation for the common features is simply that they are advantageous in terms of evolutionary theory that does not make them right.

Evolution is a blind force incapable of conferring a moral imprimatur on human behaviour. It may be a fact that concern for kin is in accord with evolutionary theory, but to say that concern for kin is therefore right would be to attempt to deduce values from facts.

If all human societies enslaved any tribe they could conquer, some freethinking moralists might still insist that slavery is wrong. They could not be said to be talking nonsense merely because they had few supporters. Similarly, then, universal support for principles of kinship and reciprocity cannot prove that these principles are in some way objectively justified.

This example illustrates the way in which ethics differs from a descriptive science. From the standpoint of ethics, whether human moral codes closely parallel one another or are extraordinarily diverse, the question of how an individual should act remains open. If you are thinking deeply about what you should do, your uncertainty will not be overcome by being told what your society thinks you should do in the circumstances in which you find yourself.

Even if you are told that virtually all other human societies agree, you may choose not to go that way. If you are told that there is great variation among human societies over what people should do in your circumstances, you may wonder whether there can be any objective answer, but your dilemma has still not been resolved.

In fact, this diversity does not rule out the possibility of an objective answer either: conceivably, most societies simply got it wrong. This, too, is something that will be taken up later in this article, for the possibility of an objective morality is one of the constant themes of ethics.

10.2 Axiology

Because "fact" symbolizes objectivity and "value" suggests subjectivity, the relationship of value to fact is of fundamental importance in developing any theory of the objectivity of value and of value judgments. Whereas such descriptive sciences as sociology, psychology, anthropology, and comparative religion all attempt to give a factual description of what is actually valued, as well as causal explanations of similarities and differences between the valuations, it remains the philosopher's task to ask about their objective validity.

The philosopher asks whether something is of value because it is desired, as subjectivists such as Perry hold, or whether it is desired because it has value, as objectivists such as Moore and Nicolai Hartmann claim. In both approaches, value judgments are assumed to have a cognitive status, and the approaches differ only on whether a value exists as a property of something independently of human interest in it or desire for it.

Non-cognitivists, on the other hand, deny the cognitive status of value judgments, holding that their main function is either emotive, as the positivist A.J. Ayer maintains, or prescriptive, as the analyst R.M. Hare holds. Existentialists, such as Jean-Paul Sartre, emphasizing freedom, decision, and choice of one's values, also appear to reject any logical or ontological connection between value and fact.

10.3 Theory of Value

Theory of Value is the philosophical study of goodness, or value, in the widest sense of these terms. Its significance lies (1) in the considerable expansion that it has given to the meaning of the term value and (2) in the unification that it has provided for the study of a variety of questions-- economic, moral, aesthetic, and even logical--that had often been considered in relative isolation.

The term "value" originally meant the worth of something, chiefly in the economic sense of exchange value, as in the work of the 18th-century political economist Adam Smith.

A broad extension of the meaning of value to wider areas of philosophical interest occurred during the 19th century under the influence of a variety of thinkers and schools: the Neo-Kantians Rudolf Hermann Lotze and Albrecht Ritschl; Friedrich Nietzsche, author of a theory of the transvaluation of all values; Alexius Meinong and Christian von Ehrenfels; and Eduard von Hartmann, philosopher of the unconscious, whose *Grundriss der Axiologie* (1909; "Outline of Axiology") first used the term in a title.

Hugo Münsterberg, often regarded as the founder of applied psychology, and Wilbur Marshall Urban, whose *Valuation, Its Nature and Laws* (1909) was the first treatise on this topic in English, introduced the movement to the United States. Ralph Barton Perry's book *General Theory of Value* (1926) has been called the magnum opus of the new approach. A value, he theorized, is "any object of any interest." Later, he explored eight "realms" of value: morality, religion, art, science, economics, politics, law, and custom.

A distinction is commonly made between instrumental and intrinsic value--between what is good as a means and what is good as an end. John Dewey, in *Human Nature and Conduct* (1922) and *Theory of Valuation* (1939), presented a pragmatic interpretation and tried to break down this distinction between means and ends, though the latter effort was more likely a way of emphasizing the point that many actual things in human life--such as health, knowledge, and virtue--are good in both senses.

Other philosophers, such as C.I. Lewis, Georg Henrik von Wright, and W.K. Frankena, have multiplied the distinctions--differentiating, for example, between instrumental value (being good for some purpose) and technical value (being good at doing something) or between contributory value (being good as part of a whole) and final value (being good as a whole).

Many different answers are given to the question "What is intrinsically good?" Hedonists say it is pleasure; Pragmatists, satisfaction, growth, or adjustment; Kantians, a good will; Humanists, harmonious self-realization; Christians, the love of God. Pluralists, such as G.E. Moore, W.D. Ross, Max Scheler, and Ralph Barton Perry, argue that there are any number of intrinsically good things. Moore, a founding father of Analytic philosophy, developed a theory of organic wholes, holding that the value of an aggregate of things depends upon how they are combined.

10.4 Twentieth century Social Science

What is seen in the 20th century is not only an intensification and spread of earlier tendencies in the social sciences but also the development of many new tendencies that, in the aggregate, make the 19th century seem by comparison one of quiet unity and simplicity in the social sciences.

In the 20th century, the processes first generated by the democratic and industrial revolutions have gone on virtually unchecked in Western society, penetrating more and more spheres of once traditional morality and culture, leaving their impress on more and more nations, regions, and localities. Equally important, perhaps in the long run far more so, is the spread of these revolutionary processes to the non-Western areas of the world.

The impact of industrialism, technology, secularism, and individualism upon peoples long accustomed to the ancient unities of tribe, local community, agriculture, and religion was first to be seen in the context of colonialism, an outgrowth of nationalism and capitalism in the West. The relations of the West to non-Western parts of the world, the whole phenomenon of the "new nations," are vital aspects of the social sciences.

So too are certain other consequences, or lineal episodes, of the two revolutions. The 20th century is the century of nationalism, mass democracy, and large-scale industrialism beyond reach of any 19th-century imagination so far as magnitude is concerned. It was the century of mass warfare, of two world wars with toll in lives and property greater perhaps than the sum total of all preceding wars in history.

It was the century too of totalitarianism: Communist, Fascist, and Nazi; and of techniques of terrorism that, if not novel, are to be seen on a scale and with an intensity of scientific application that could scarcely have been predicted by those who considered science and technology as unqualifiedly humane in possibility. It is a century of affluence in the West, without precedent for the masses of people, to be seen in a constantly rising standard of living and a constantly rising level of expectations.

The last is important. A great deal of the turbulence in the 20th century-- political, economic, and social--was the result of desires and aspirations that have been constantly escalating and that have been passing from the white people in the West to ethnic and racial minorities among them and, then, to whole continents elsewhere.

Of all manifestations of revolution, the revolution of rising expectations is perhaps the most powerful in its consequences. For, once this revolution gets under way, each fresh victory in the struggle for rights, freedom, and security tends to magnify the importance of what has not been won.

10.5 Social structure

Several ideas of social change have been developed in various cultures and historical periods. Three of them may be distinguished as the most basic: (1) the idea of decline or degeneration, or, in religious terms, the fall from an original state of grace; (2) the idea of cyclical change, a pattern of subsequent and recurring phases of growth and decline; and (3) the idea of continuous progress. These three ideas were already prominent in Greek and Roman antiquity and have characterized Western social thought from that time.

The concept of progress, however, became the most influential idea, especially since the 18th-century Enlightenment. Social thinkers like Anne-Robert-Jacques Turgot and the Marquis de Condorcet in France and Adam Smith and John Millar in Scotland advanced theories on the progress of human knowledge and technology.

Progress was the key idea in 19th-century theories of social evolution, and evolutionism was the common core shared by the most influential social theories of the century. Evolutionism implied that mankind as a whole progresses along one line of development; that this development is predetermined and inevitable, since it corresponds to definite laws; that some societies are more advanced in this development than other ones; and that Western society is the most advanced and therefore indicates the future of the rest of mankind. Auguste Comte, a French philosopher and sociologist, advanced a "law of three stages," according to which mankind progresses from a theological stage, which is dominated by religion, through a metaphysical stage, in which abstract speculative thinking is most prominent, and onward toward a positivist stage, in which scientific theories based on empirical research come to dominate.

The most encompassing theory of social evolution was developed by Herbert Spencer, who, unlike Comte, linked social evolution to biological evolution. According to Spencer, biological organisms and human societies follow the same universal, natural evolutionary law: "a change from a state of relatively indefinite, incoherent, homogeneity to a state of relatively definite, coherent, heterogeneity." In other words, as societies grow in size, they become more complex; their parts differentiate, specialize into different functions, and become, consequently, more interdependent.

Evolutionary thought also dominated the new field of social and cultural anthropology in the second half of the 19th century. Anthropologists such as Sir Edward Burnett Tylor and Lewis Henry Morgan classified contemporary societies on an evolutionary scale. Morgan ranked them from "savage" through "barbarian" to "civilized." Tylor postulated an evolution of religious ideas from animism through polytheism to monotheism. Morgan classified societies on the basis of the level of technology, or sources of subsistence, which he connected with the kinship system. He assumed that monogamy was preceded by polygamy, and patrilineal descent by matrilineal descent.

10.6 Background of primate studies

The inclusion of man in the order provides the rationale for the vigour with which this group has been studied by scientists since the time of Galen of Pergamum. Aristotle and Hippocrates, in the 3rd and 4th centuries BC, recognized the similarity of man and apes, but it was Galen who demonstrated the truth of this kinship by dissection. He wrote, "the ape is likest to man in viscera, muscles, arteries, veins, nerves and in the form of bones."

It should be noted that Galen was in fact referring to monkeys, not the true apes, which were unknown to western man until the 15th century. None of these early scientists saw any evolutionary significance in the similarity of man and "apes," a correspondence that they regarded as purely coincidental. An inkling of the truth of man's relationship with primates must have penetrated the mind of St. Albertus Magnus, probably the best leading naturalist of the Middle Ages, who produced a classification of animal life in his book *De animalibus*. Albertus' classification, which placed man between "apes" (monkeys) on the one hand and "animals" on the other, provides the first whiff of the "missing-link" concept, which later was to befog the issue of man's place in nature.

The Dark Ages were aptly named as far as knowledge of primates is concerned. The first evidence of a renaissance of interest was in the time of Vesalius, the great Belgian anatomist of the 16th century, who published a comparative anatomy of man and "apes" in order to confound the precepts of Galen. He did not succeed in disproving Galen's assertion that "apes were likest to man" but, unwittingly, he succeeded in stirring up an interest in the biology of primates that has never since flagged. The first true ape studied as a scientific specimen was a chimpanzee dissected by Edward Tyson, an English anatomist, in 1699.

Tyson's specimen, which he called the "Orang-Outang, sive Homo Sylvestris," is to this day housed in the British Museum (Natural History), mounted in a standing position that reflects Tyson's belief that he had discovered the pygmy, a race of humans known since the time of the ancient Greeks. Tyson wrote of his "pygmie" that it was "no man, nor yet a common ape but a sort of animal between both." It never occurred to Tyson or his contemporaries, who believed that all animals had been created independently in their current image, that man, apes, and monkeys were connected by common evolutionary descent. In 1758, Linnaeus--the father of animal and plant classification--added the lemurs and bats to the monkeys, apes, and man and called the whole assemblage the Primates.

It is to be noted, however, that Linnaeus was sufficiently perceptive to see that man was a primate. His conclusion was regarded as a grave blow to human dignity, and it was followed by new classifications such as that of

Blumenbach in 1776, placing man in a separate order. Man was not again considered part of the primate order until a century later when the English anatomist St. George Mivart in the climate of post-Darwinian thought published his classification of primates.

The first evolutionist was a French scholar of the late 18th century, the Chevalier de Lamarck, who saw animal life as an uninterrupted continuity in which old species were transformed into new species in a sequence of increasing complexity and perfection. In 1821 Baron Georges Cuvier, a rabid anti-evolutionist, had the historic distinction of describing *Adapis*, the first fossil primate genus ever recognized. Fossils such as *Adapis*, Cuvier believed, were the remains of animals destroyed by past catastrophes (floods, earthquakes, etc.) and living animals were new stocks divinely created to fill the vacuum, a view consistent with the widely held notion that species were immutable.

During the early 19th century a number of geologists and biologists questioned the doctrine of immutability, but it was not until 1859, with the publication of Charles Darwin's "On the Origin of Species by Means of Natural Selection," that positive evidence was provided, along with a sound alternative theory. The Darwinian contention that not only had man evolved, but he had evolved from a simian ancestor resulted in acrimonious debate among scientists, theologians, philosophers, and laymen.

As influential zoologists and anatomists rose to support Darwin, the truth of man's primate consanguinity began to be accepted, if not actually relished. Today, few scientists deny that man and the lower primates belong in the same order; in fact, much current research is directed toward closing the apparent gap between the highest of the nonhuman primates, the chimpanzee and gorilla, and man.

In times past, the public image of primates was largely dictated by prevailing religious beliefs. In Asian countries, where primates abound, monkeys have for a long time been regarded with various degrees of deference that, among Hindus in India, for instance, amounts to worship.

In Europe and North America, where monkeys and apes are totally absent, no religious sect has attached divine significance to them and, in fact, the reverse has been the case, monkeys at various times having been regarded as the personification of evil and depravity, familiars of the devil. This image, however, is fading as a result of enlightened instruction in schools and the advances in naturalistic presentation of primates in zoos. The nonhuman primate is becoming generally accepted by laymen as an animal of peculiar interest to man with many amusing and endearing qualities.

The qualities of primates, however, are less endearing to farmers and agriculturists in certain parts of the world. In South Africa, the chacma baboon (*Papio ursinus*) competes with domestic sheep for grazing lands and is an occasional predator of lambs; in West and Central Africa native crops are subject to daily assaults by forest-living monkeys; and, in India, macaques, which have been accorded a semi-sacred status, live alongside man in towns and villages and are parasitic upon him for their food and shelter.

Scientific interest in nonhuman primates, their structure at all levels and their way of life, is currently in the ascendancy. Their value as research animals increases year by year, so that at present over a quarter of a million wild monkeys are consumed annually by laboratories in the study of human diseases, in the production of vaccines, in the experiments of organ transplantation, in the testing of drugs and, even, for the clinical trials of new cosmetics.

Clearly their scientific usefulness raises important problems of conservation of primate stocks in the wild. Other disciplines whose researches depend upon observations and upon experimentation with nonhuman primates include those of endocrinology, neurology, psychology, and sociology. Much is being learned as a result of such study that is of great significance for man and his future betterment.

10.7 Social class

Class is a group of people within a society who possess the same socioeconomic status. Besides being important in social theory, the concept of class as a collection of individuals sharing similar economic circumstances has been widely used in censuses and in studies of social mobility.

The term "class" first came into wide use in the early 19th century, replacing such terms as rank and order as descriptions of the major hierarchical groupings in society. The usage reflected changes in the structure of western European societies after the industrial and political revolutions of the late 18th century. Feudal distinctions of rank were declining in importance, and the new social groups that were developing-- the commercial and industrial capitalists and the urban working class in the new factories--were defined mainly in economic terms, by the ownership of capital, on one side, or dependence on wages, on the other.

Though the term "class" has been applied to social groups in a wide range of societies, including ancient city-states, early empires, and caste or feudal societies, it is most usefully confined to the social divisions in modern societies, particularly industrialized ones. Social classes must be distinguished from status groups; the former are based primarily upon economic interests, while the latter are constituted by evaluations of the honour or prestige of an occupation, cultural position, or family descent.

Theories of social class were only fully elaborated in the 19th century as the modern social sciences, especially sociology, developed. Such political philosophers as Thomas Hobbes, John Locke, and Jean-Jacques Rousseau discussed the issues of social inequality and stratification, and French and English writers in the late 18th and early 19th centuries put forth the idea that the non-political elements in society, such as the economic system and the family, largely determined a society's form of political life.

This idea was taken further by the French social theorist Henri de Saint-Simon, who argued that a state's form of government corresponded with the character of the underlying system of economic production. In the writings of Saint-Simon's successors, there first appeared a theory of the proletariat, or urban working class, as a major political force in modern society, and this directly influenced the development of Karl Marx's theory.

Marx's theory of class has dominated all later discussion of the topic. According to Marx, what distinguishes one type of society from another is its mode of production (i.e., the nature of its technology and division of labour), and each mode of production engenders a distinctive class system in which one class controls and directs the process of production while another class is, or other classes are, the direct producers and the providers of services to the dominant class.

The relations between the classes are antagonistic, since they are in conflict over the appropriation of what is produced; and in certain periods, when the mode of production itself is changing as a result of developments in technology and in the utilization of labour, such conflicts become extreme and a new class challenges the dominance of the existing rulers of society.

The dominant class controls not only material production but also the production of ideas; it thus establishes a particular cultural style and a dominant political doctrine, and its control over society is consolidated in a particular type of political system. Subject classes that are growing in strength and influence as a result of changes in the mode of production generate political doctrines and movements in opposition to the ruling class.

The theory of class is at the centre of Marx's social theory, for it is the social classes formed within a particular mode of production that are regarded as establishing a particular form of state, animating political conflicts, and bringing about major changes in the structure of society.

Subsequent theories of class have mainly been concerned to revise, refute, or provide an alternative to Marxist theory. The German sociologist Max

Weber questioned the importance of social classes in the political development of modern societies, pointing out religious mores, nationalism, and other factors as playing a role as well. But Marxist theory's emphasis on the importance of class conflict--*i.e.*, on conflict and struggle between the classes for control of the means of production--has been the most controversial issue dividing social theorists in their analysis of class structure.

Many of those opposed to Marxist theory have focused attention on the functional interdependence of different classes and their harmonious collaboration with each other. And indeed, by the late 20th century it seemed undeniable that the classes in capitalist societies have tended to lose their distinctive character, while the antagonism between them has declined to such an extent that in most economically advanced countries it no longer produces serious political conflict.

Moreover, Marxism's prediction of the proletariat's successful revolution against the bourgeoisie and its replacement of the capitalist system by a classless society have rung increasingly hollow in light of the dismal record of most 20th-century Marxist governments and their wholesale collapse from internal causes between 1989 and 1991.

Despite controversies over the theory of class, there is general agreement among social scientists on the characteristics of the principal social classes in modern societies. Sociologists generally posit three classes: upper, working (or lower), and middle.

The upper class in modern capitalist societies is distinguished above all by the possession of largely inherited wealth. In the United States, for example, more than 30 percent of all wealth is concentrated in the hands of the top 1 percent of property owners. The ownership of large amounts of property and the income derived from it confer many advantages upon the members of the upper class. They are able to develop a distinctive style of life based on extensive cultural pursuits and leisure activities, to exert a considerable influence on economic policy and political decisions, and to procure for their children a superior education and economic opportunities that help to perpetuate family wealth.

The principal contrast with the upper class in industrial societies is provided by the working class, which traditionally consisted of manual workers in the extractive and manufacturing industries. Given the vast expansion of the service sector in the world's most advanced economies, it is necessary to broaden this definition to include in the working class those persons who hold low-paying, low-skilled, non-unionized jobs in such service industries as food service and retail sales.

There are considerable differences within the working class, however, and a useful distinction exists between skilled, semiskilled, and unskilled workers that broadly correspond with differences in income level. What characterizes the working class as a whole is lack of property and dependence on wages. Associated with this condition are relatively low living standards, restricted access to higher education, and exclusion, to a large extent, from the spheres of important decision making.

Aside from the dramatic rise in living standards that occurred in the decades after World War II, the main factor affecting the working class in the second half of the 20th century was a general shift in the economy from manufacturing to service industries, involving a contraction in the numbers of manual workers. In the United States and Great Britain, among other countries, the decline in traditional manufacturing industries left a core of chronically unemployed persons isolated from the economic mainstream in decaying urban areas. This new urban substratum of permanently jobless and underemployed workers has been termed the underclass by some sociologists.

The middle class may be said to include the middle and upper levels of clerical workers, those engaged in technical and professional occupations, supervisors and managers, and such self-employed workers as small-scale shopkeepers, businessmen, and farmers. At the top--in the case of wealthy professionals or managers in large corporations--the middle class merges into the upper class, while at the bottom--where routine and poorly paid jobs in sales, distribution, and transport are concerned--it merges into the working class.

It seems clear that rising living standards in Western industrial societies after 1945 and changes in social policy that resulted in the provision of more elaborate welfare services have generated significant changes in the class system. A general diminution of class differences has resulted from higher standards of living, greater social mobility, and a limited redistribution of wealth and income.

These changes were generally reflected in a decline of class ideologies and class conflict. The middle class, which rose to dominance in Western capitalist societies in the 19th and 20th centuries, consolidated its position in the decades after World War II, and this process was being repeated in the expanding economies of Japan and other East and Southeast Asian countries in the late 20th century.

11. HUMAN NATURE

11.1 Human beings in groups

People live in groups, in a society, because they get something from it. This in fact is the simple definition of sociology and what human nature is.

The concept of human nature is a common part of everyday thought. The ordinary person feels that he comes to know human nature through the character and conduct of the people he meets. Behind what they do he recognizes qualities that often do not surprise him: he forms expectations as to the sort of qualities possessed by other human beings and about the ways they differ from, for example, dogs or horses.

People are proud, sensitive, eager for recognition or admiration, often ambitious, hopeful or despondent, and selfish or capable of self-sacrifice. They take satisfaction in their achievements, have within them something called a conscience, and are loyal or disloyal.

11.2 Observing people

Experience in dealing with and observing people gives rise to a conception of a predictable range of conduct; conduct falling outside the range that is considered not to be worthy of a human is frequently regarded as inhuman or bestial whereas that which is exceptional--in that it lives up to standards which most people recognize but few achieve--is regarded as superhuman or saintly.

The common conception of human nature thus implicitly locates man on a scale of perfection, placing him somewhere above most animals but below saints, prophets, or angels. This idea was embodied in the theme, Hellenic in origin, of the Great Chain of Being--a hierarchical order ascending from the most simple and inert to the most complex and active: mineral, vegetable, animal, man, and finally divine beings superior to man.

In the Middle Ages these divine beings constituted the various orders of angels, with God as the single, supremely perfect and omnipotent, ever-active being.

There was a tendency in this theory to take for granted the commonality among all human beings, something by virtue of which they could be classified as fully human, which differentiates them from all other animals, and which gives them their place in the order of things. Yet, as with many notions that are habitually employed, the request for a precise definition of "human nature" proves highly problematic.

11.3 Notion of form and nature

The Greeks--most notably Plato and Aristotle--introduced the notion of form, nature, or essence as an explanatory, metaphysical concept. Variations on this concept were central to Western thought until the 17th century. Observation of the natural world raised the question of why creatures reproduced after their kind and could not be interbred at will and of why, for example, acorns grew into oaks and not into roses.

To explain such phenomena it was postulated that the seeds, whether plant or animal, must each already contain within them the form, nature, or essence of the species from which they were derived and into which they would subsequently develop. This pattern of explanation is preserved in the modern biological concept of a genetic code that is embodied in the DNA molecular structure of each cell. There are important differences, however, between the modern concept of a genetic code and the older, Greek-derived concept of form or essence.

First, biologists are now able to locate, isolate, experimentally analyze, and manipulate DNA molecules in what has become known as genetic engineering. Being the structures responsible for physical development, DNA molecules represent the terms by which man can be biologically characterized. Forms or essences, on the other hand, were not observable; if they were granted any independent existence, it was as immaterial entities.

The form, nature, or essence of man or of any other kind of being was posited as a principle present in the thing, determining its kind by producing in it an innate tendency to strive to develop into a perfect example of itself--to fulfil its nature and to realize its full potential as a thing of a given kind. This gave rise to a teleological, or purposive, view of the natural world in which developments were explained by reference to the goal toward which each natural thing, by its nature, strives; *i.e.,* by reference to the ideal form it seeks to realize. By contrast, the genetic structure present in each cell is now invoked to explain the subsequent development of an organism in a "mechanistic" and non-purposive way, in which development is shown to be dependent upon and determined by pre-existing structures and conditions.

Second, genetic mutability forms an essential part of modern evolutionary biology. Not only are there genetic differences between individuals of a given species to account for differences between them in features, such as coloration, but random genetic mutation in the presence of changing environmental conditions may result in alterations to the genetic constitution of the species as a whole. Thus, in evolutionary biological theory species are not stable; natural kinds do not have the fixed, immutable forms or essences characteristic of biology before the advent of evolutionary theory.

Within either framework, if human nature is understood simply as man's special form of that which is biologically inherited in all species, there remains the delicate problem of discovering, in any given case, exactly what role environment plays in determining the actual characteristics of mature members of the species. Even in the case of purely physiological characteristics this may be far from straightforward: for example, the extent to which diet, exercise, and conditions of work determine such things as susceptibility to heart disease and cancer remains the subject of intensive scientific investigation.

11.4 Psychological characteristics

In the case of behavioural and psychological characteristics, such as intelligence, the problems are multiplied to the point where they are no longer problems that can be answered by purely empirical investigation. There is room for much conceptual debate about what is meant by intelligence and over what tests, if any, can be supposed to yield a direct measure of this capacity, and thus provide evidence that an individual's level of intelligence is determined at birth (by nature) rather than by subsequent exposure to the environment (nurture) that conditions the development of all his capacities.

This debate--whether the variation in intelligence levels is a product of the conditions into which people all having the same initial potential are born, or whether it is a reflection of variations in the capacities with which they are born--is very closely related to the question of whether there is such a thing as human nature common to all human beings, or whether there are intrinsic differences among those whom we recognize as belonging to the biological species *Homo sapiens*. This is because, as the name *Homo sapiens* suggests, man is traditionally thought to be distinguished from and privileged above other animals by virtue of his possession of reason, or intellect.

When the intellect is positively valued as that which is distinctively human and which confers superiority on man, the thought that different races of people differ by nature in their intellectual capacities has been used as a justification for a variety of racist attitudes and policies.

Those of another race, of supposedly lesser intellectual development, are classified as less than fully human and therefore as needing to be accorded less than full human rights. Similarly, the thought that women are by nature intellectually inferior to men has been used as a justification for their domination by men, for refusing them education, and even for according them the legal status of property owned by men.

On the other hand, if differences in adult intellectual capacity are regarded as a product of the circumstances in which potentially similar people are brought up, the attitude is to consider all as equally human but some as having been more privileged when growing up than others.

More radically, the evidence for variations in intelligence levels may be questioned by challenging the objectivity of the standards relative to which these levels are assessed. It may be argued that conceptions of what constitutes a rational or intelligent response to a situation or to a problem are themselves culturally conditioned, a product of the way in which the members of the group devising the tests and making the judgments have themselves been taught to think.

Such an argument has the effect of undermining claims by any one human group to intellectual superiority over others, whether these others be their contemporaries or their own forebears. Hence, they may also be used to discredit any idea of a progressive development of human intellectual capacities.

These debates about intelligence and rationality provide an example of the complexity of the impact of evolutionary biology on conceptions of human nature, for the dominant traditions in Western thought about human nature have tended to concentrate attention more on what distinguishes man from other animals than on the strictly biological constitution that he largely shares with them. Possession of reason or intellect is far from being the only candidate considered for such a distinguishing characteristic.

1.5 Man, the tool user

Man has been characterized as essentially a tool user, or fabricator (Homo faber), as essentially social, as essentially a language user, and so on. These represent differing views concerning the fundamental feature that gives rise to all the other qualities regarded as distinctively human and which serve to mark man off from other animals. These characteristics all centre on mental, intellectual, psychological--i.e., non-physiological--characteristics and thus leave scope for debate about the relation between mind and body.

So long as this question remains open, and so long as mental or intellectual constitution remains the central consideration in discussions of human nature, the question of changes in--and of the possible evolution of--human nature will remain relatively independent of those devoted to physiological change and hence of strictly biological evolution.

Until the 15th century the standard assumption was that man had a fixed nature, one that determined both his place in the universe and his destiny. The Renaissance humanists, however, proclaimed that what distinguishes man from all other creatures is that he has no nature. This was a way of asserting that man's actions are not bound by laws of nature in the way that those of other creatures are. Man is capable of taking responsibility for his own actions because he has the freedom to exercise his will. This view received two subsequent interpretations.

First, the human character is indefinitely plastic; each individual is given determinate form by the environment in which he is born, brought up, and lives. In this case, changes or developments in human beings will be regarded as the product of social or cultural changes, changes that themselves are often more rapid than biological evolution.

11.6 History, politics and sociology

It is thus to disciplines such as history, politics, and sociology, rather than to biology, that one should look for an understanding of these processes. But if disciplines such as these must constitute the primary study of man, then the question of the extent to which this can be a strictly scientific study arises. The methods of history are not, and cannot be, those of the natural sciences. And the legitimacy of the claims of the so-called social or human sciences to genuine scientific status has frequently been called into question and remains a focus for debate.

Second, each individual is autonomous and must "make" himself. Assertion of the autonomy of man involves rejection of the possibility of discovering laws of human behaviour or of the course of history, for freedom is precisely not being bound by law, by nature. In this case, the study of man can never be parallel to the natural sciences with their theoretical structures based on the discovery of laws of nature.

END

12. BIBLIOGRAPHY

1. MORAL PHILOSOPHY, FROM SOCRATES TO THE 21ST AEON, ISBN: 978-1-4457-4618-0
2. MORAL PHILOSOPHY, FROM HIPPOCRATES TO THE 21ST AEON, ISBN: 978-1-84753-463-7
3. THERAPEUTIC PHILOSOPHY FOR THE INDIVIDUAL AND THE STATE, ISBN: 978-1-4092-7586-2
4. PHILOSOPHIC COUNSELLING FOR PEOPLE AND THEIR GOVERNMENTS, ISBN: 978-1-4092-7400-1
5. MORAL PHILOSOPHY, THE ETHICAL APPROACH THROUGH THE AGES, ISBN: 978-1-4092-7703-3
6. MORAL PHILOSOPHY, ISBN: 978-1-4478-5037-3
7. PSYCHOANALYSIS, POETRY, ISBN: 978-1-4467-2741-6
8. PLATO'S EPISTEMOLOGY, ISBN: 978-1-4716-6584-4
9. ARISTOTLE'S AETIOLOGY, ISBN: 978-1-4716-7861-5
10. MARXISM, SOCIALISM & COMMUNISM, ISBN: 978-1-4716-8236-0
11. MACHIAVELLI'S POLITICS & RELEVANT PHILOSOPHICAL CONCEPTS, ISBN: 978-1-4716-8629-0
12. BRITISH PHILOSOPHERS, 16TH TO 18TH CENTURY, ISBN: 978-1-4717-1072-8
13. ROUSSEAU ON WILL AND MORALITY, ISBN: 978-1-4717-1070-4
14. HEGEL ON IDEALISM, KNOWLEDGE & REALITY, ISBN: 978-1-4717-0954-8
15. PHILOLOGY, CONCEPTS OF EUROPEAN LITERATURE, ISBN: 978-1-291-49148-7
16. THREE MILLENNIA OF HELLENIC PHILOLOGY, ISBN: 978-1291-49799-1
17. CYPRUS, PERMANENT DEPRIVATION OF FREEDOM, ISBN: 978-1-291-50833-8
18. MEDICAL ETHICS THROUGH THE AGES, ISBN: 978-1-4092- 7468-1
19. MEDICAL ETHICS, FROM HIPPOCRATES TO THE 21ST CENTURY ISBN: 978-1-4457-1203-1
20. THE MISINTERPRETATION OF SIGMUND FREUD, ISBN: 978-1-4467-1659-5
21. JUNG'S PSYCHOTHERAPY: THE PSYCHOLOGICAL & MYTHOLOGICAL METHODS, ISBN: 978-1-4477-4740-6
22. FREUDIAN ANALYSIS & JUNGIAN SYNTHESIS, ISBN: 978-1-4477-5996-6
23. PSYCHOLOGY FROM CONCEPTION TO SENILITY, ISBN: 978-1-4092-7218-2
24. PSYCHOTHERAPY, CONCEPTS OF TREATMENT, ISBN: 978-1-291-50178-0
25. PSYCHOLOGY, CONCEPTS OF BEHAVIOUR, ISBN: 978-1-291-47573-9
26. PSYCHOLOGY OF CHILD CULTURE, ISBN: 978-1-4092-7619-7
27. JOYFUL PARENTING, ISBN: 0 9527956 1 2
28. THE GUIDE TO A JOYFUL PARENTING, ISBN: 0 952 7956 1 2
29. PHILOSOPHY FOR HUMAN BEHAVIOUR, ISBN: 978-1-291-12707-2
30. SOCIOLOGY, CONCEPTS OF GROUP BEHAVIOUR, ISBN: 978-1-291-51888-7